The Unseen

The Unseen

How Positive Thoughts and Feelings define Potential
and impacts your Reality

By Moriam S. Balogun

Interior design: Moriam S. Balogun

ISBN 978-1523267453
ISBN 1523267453

Have faith in The Unseen

As a thank you for reading this book, I'd like to offer you some extra tools to help you build the life of your dreams.

On my website you will find a number of helpful tools to support the information given within each chapter. As an extra gift, I would like to offer you a limited edition guided manifestation creation meditation, to help you supercharge your focus and create the life you desire consciously.

Just visit www.theunseen.net/free to get these transformation tools today.

❦ Table of Contents ❧

○3 Preface ○

The world in which we live is a living, breathing, thinking, feeling universe. Its appearance is as it appears to you or I, but will differ depending on our individual perspectives. What you see and experience in life is governed by what you expect to see. It can be no other way. You will never see or experience anything in your life which you do not think is possible.

Your reality of life - that is, how you expect life to be and, therefore, how it manifests for you - is spiritually and scientifically reliant upon your thoughts, feelings and emotions. This has been noted in every religious book, signified by every deity and preached by many a spiritual teacher. So, not only does religion state this, science confirms this too. Neuroscience and quantum physics state that our realities are shaped by our beliefs, perceptions and perspectives. This statement will either fill you with joy or make you cringe. Again, this will depend on your particular perspective of life.

Your role in this universe is to play the part of Observer and Experiencer and as an individual expression of this universe, of which we are part, to live accordingly. What could this mean? Many people believe in the concept of God as something which is greater than all of us. Some will call this concept the universal intelligence, source or the divine. Whichever name you give to it or whichever label you resonate with is subject to your own belief system, but one thing which is certain - regardless of its name – is that we are all connected to it. If this is the case, then in some way, we are all individual expressions of the universe, each with free will. Free will means we may choose what our experiences are. We may decide how we wish to live our lives and through consciousness (an understanding of the world around us) we may then create our world as we see fit. The question is 1) How many of us do this with the full scope of our consciousness? and 2) Do we really understand what this means, and what the consequences of that full consciousness could be?

❦ Prologue ❧

This universe is as much physical (matter) as non-physical (energy), and both these elements are of equal importance in understanding the world around us. At the turn of the 17th century, Newtonian science led us to believe in the theory of cause and effect. In short, cause and effect means that nothing happens by chance and that everything that happens has a physical cause. The theory describes the relationship between one event and another, action and reaction. Looking at this theory from the perspective of there being only matter, as Isaac Newton strongly believed, this theory could be proven and would be absolutely correct.

However, in the 20th century, scientists such as Albert Einstein (Theory of Relativity, E=mc2), Niels Bohr (Bohr Model of the Atom), Max Planck (Quantum Theory) and Erwin Schrödinger (Schrödinger's Cat Theory), proved that life as we knew it was not only a question of matter, but at a microscopic level, a question of energy too. When we place particles (matter) under a microscope, we discover at its most minute level an undeniable energy field. Matter and energy are intrinsically tied together. Without energy there can be no matter and without matter energy cannot materialize.

Energy can be recognized within particles or as wave forms. For example, we can observe the energy emitted from heat by looking at heat waves on the horizon, on a hot day. Energy itself is not visible to the human eye, although some people are able to see aura's – the energy flow surrounded or emitted from living creatures. Taking the example of energy in the form of heat waves, we know that an object may be very warm simply by placing our hands near, for example, a pan on a hot stove. We don't necessarily have to see the heat energy produced by a warm pan, but by placing our hands close to it, we are able to feel the energy emitted and know that energy exists.

Now, if the underlying basis of everything consists of both particles AND energy, then the theory of cause and effect, as Newton described, is not correct. If physical events are fundamentally energetic at their core, could this mean that energy is responsible for the manifestation of physical outcomes?

If realities are inherently created at an energetic level, (think of waves, for example), then it's quite possible that our thoughts or emotions (which are predominantly energetic and transmitted through waveform), play a major role in how the world exists. When we look at cause (action) and effect (reaction) in the Newtonian sense and bring in the 20th century discoveries by Einstein et al, then we can conclude that the theory of cause and effect must now become the theory of effect and cause. In other words, our thoughts have influence (effect) and our realities are the physical materializations (cause).This understanding changes just about everything we understand about our world and requires a paradigm shift.

The undeniable field of energy, The Unseen, scientifically known as the Quantum Field, exists within all matter. Everything in our world is made up of particles (matter) and therefore, at its deepest level, made up of The Unseen. It has been described as the field of potential where all probabilities exist and where anything is possible. The Unseen is omnipresent and omnipotent. It is an energy field that can never be destroyed but can change, transmute, transcend and resonate.

This energy is the energy of the universe, the energy of **ALL THINGS** and something which exists as a part of and within us all. That what exists in The Unseen, our thoughts, feelings, and emotions, creates our physical realities. **We create our world by the power of how we feel about certain thoughts**. What we think about, on a deep subconscious level, is what we manifest.

How we affect our lives depends on how much access we have to The Unseen. If The Unseen contains all potential and all possibilities, then the options and choices we have are limitless. When we understand this, we see that we have much more power and potential than ever thought possible. Potential is not something which is available to only some. Nor is it subject to who you are, which race you belong to, which country you live in or what kind of background

you have. Infinite potential is available to all those of us who are willing to tap into the power of The Unseen.

This book is not for the lazy minded. We live in a living, breathing, thinking, feeling universe; but more so, we live in an active (*doing*) universe. This means that we may not just sit and wait for our desires to turn into the realities. As you will see, we need to foster positive feelings and take positive actions. The idea that positive thinking will change your life in a whim is naïve. Although it will help to have a positive perspective on things, positive thinking alone simply will not do. It is through this kind of thinking and belief than many unsuccessfully implement the Laws of Attraction and presume that it does not work. In order to tune into the potential of The Unseen and create the life you really desire and deserve, you must be prepared to work, think, act, dream, feel and emotionalize your life in the direction of your dreams.

Action steps will include:

- Understanding how your thoughts form your feelings and thus connect to The Unseen, affecting you in both good and bad ways

- Getting to grips with habits that no longer serve you and replacing them with ones that do

- Identifying the thoughts and patterns you do solely out of conditioning

- Visualizing your life differently from what you physically see and

- Releasing much of what you THINK you know about how life is and learning to adopt a new vision

To get the most out of this book you must take action and responsibility. If you want to create the life you desire you must

realize that everything you see in your life is a direct reflection of everything you have imagined your life to be, and everything you have been brought up and conditioned to believe.

Failure to understand this is failure in understanding the basic principles of The Unseen. You don't have to agree; you don't even have to like the way the universe works. But you cannot avoid it.

Changing your life means making a fundamental change in YOU!

If you are willing to do the work, with this book's help, and self-reflection and action, you will start to:

- Create real happiness
- Learn how to listen and trust your intuition
- Learn how to have faith in the future
- Manifest all the things you want in your life
- Find the dream job you may be looking for
- Improve your finances and income
- Create more success in your life
- Find inner peace
- Improve the quality of your life
- Live a life without fear

This book strives to illustrate how The Unseen works and how you can utilize it to bring success and happiness into your life. Through real-life examples with subjects such as our relationship to money, love, and work, descriptions have been included of how The Unseen affects these areas and how we are able to influence and live our highest and best lives possible.

Much of the science has been left out of this book, but references have been included in the event you want to delve into the studies and background behind this truth.

My advice to you is to read the book at first in its entirety, and then choose any individual chapters that you would like to work on.

PROLOGUE

Use the book as a reference guide. It contains information which can't always be digested and implemented in one go. Remember, you are making steps to change your life and this means working through many years of habit, possible negative thinking and conditioning. The changes may not happen overnight, although this is certainly imaginable. Everything is possible in our world of potentiality. Make the most of it.

I wish you goodness, abundance, experience and joy on this new journey of deliberate creation in your life. Have faith in The Unseen.

❧ Chapter 1 ☙
Faith And The Art Of Positive Experiences

Introduction

As children, we imagined goblins and dragons, spaceships and astronauts. We jumped from sofa to sofa to escape the burning lava with our siblings. We were innocent and unafraid with an unwavering sense of invincibility.

As we got older, we were taught to be careful and afraid. We were taught that badness was lurking throughout the world. We learned to be fearful and justified it as a form of self-protection. In the process we stopped dreaming, imagining, playing and loving unconditionally. We become adults, mature, sensible and 'realistic' because that's what happens when we grow up. That's what we're supposed to do. That's what everyone does. And then life happens....

You're most likely reading this book because you've come to a point or realization that your life isn't what you want it to be. The fact that you are questioning it means that some level of awareness or consciousness has awakened within you and you are now looking within. Looking within means looking at that which can't be seen with our physical eyes. We are essentially looking at The Unseen and discovering that we have been tapping into this infinite source to arrive at where we are today.

Explanation

Faith is a cornerstone to tapping into that source. The ability to have faith is one of the underlying principles of getting life to go your way. Faith is reliant on our ability to see that which is not physically visible. We tap into our faith system through the power of our thoughts and emotions and through these senses we have access to The Unseen. As the Law of Attraction states, anything you think about you bring about. The energies of your thoughts and emotions communicate with The Unseen.

We have approximately 60.000 thoughts running through our heads every day. And with those thoughts are emotions and feelings attached to them. Our thoughts determine our emotions. How we feel is the direct translation of what we are thinking. Sometimes our thoughts can be strong and intense, and at other times subtle and barely recognizable. This means that our feelings can also be subtle, but in either case they are always there.

The Unseen is unbiased. It can't think for you. It will act regardless of whether your thoughts and feelings are pleasant or unpleasant. Energy is always transmitted even if it's to your detriment, such as a negative thought about yourself, an event or even someone else. This is why we need to be conscious about what kind of thoughts we allow into our minds. When we think about upsetting circumstances or situations, we emit the same depth of faith towards it as when we are thinking about positive things.

Example

Let me give you an example of faith at work. Let's say you've just had a job interview. It went well. You had a great meeting with your potential new boss and have a good idea of what it would be like to work there. Now, let's take it a step further. After your meeting, you depart and on the way home you imagine, in the depths of your mind, yourself working there and talking to colleagues. You also see yourself in meetings, talking to clients, etc. You seem to have a good feeling about the interview even though you've not officially been offered the job yet. You just "know" that you stand a good chance of being hired.

In the above example, what's actually happening is that you have created a vision in your mind. You can see yourself at this new place of work, with colleagues, etc. and you are unconsciously tapping into The Unseen to create a new reality. This vision sends an impression to The Unseen. It sees it as a physical event that you want to create. Though your vision and imagination you are dictating what you want to manifest. Simply stated, you are informing The Unseen that you want the job because your vision contains images and feelings of you doing the job. A week or so later you are offered the job. It could be no other way.

If we analyze the above example, then we can understand how this job was manifested through the power of faith and positive expectation. The primary reasons why you were offered the job are:

1) You felt confident about your ability to do the work (energy)
2) You had a great interview where you built rapport (energy)
3) You tapped into The Unseen by fusing enthusiasm, good feelings and positive thoughts. (thought and energy)

This is The Unseen working in perfect harmony with the energy of your desires. The Unseen contains all the potential you put into it. It contains all the possibilities you imagine and it is the Law of Attraction that is used to communicate with it. The above example is the exact way how The Unseen gives you what you desire.

Scenario

Now, let's take an example of how you may bring about a negative consequence through The Unseen and Law of Attraction. Let's look at that same interview example. This time, you aren't feeling so confident about it. Let's say the interview went well but you have doubts about your skills or yourself in general. You feel insecure. In your vision you see yourself working there, but other thoughts start to creep in. You imagine certain colleagues won't like you. Or, you imagine you have to fight for recognition and have to prove yourself with clients. In other words, you imagine struggling. As you go home, this vision continues to run at a subconscious level through your thoughts and this is what you are communicating, via the Law of Attraction, to The Unseen. One thought leads to another and you are creating more doubts and insecurities. Before you know it, you've convinced yourself that you won't be able to do the job.

In this scenario, you've told yourself AND The Unseen that you don't want the job. Not directly, but indirectly. You've communicated this through your thoughts and feelings of the interview by focusing on the possible struggles you experience. When we focus

in such a way on future events, we are focusing and calling in that exact possibility or potential. The potential which The Unseen holds are the thoughts that you imagine and the emotions that you feel. This will become the reality you create for yourself and is what The Unseen will deliver. The Law of Attraction is unbiased, which means it will always transmit from you what you strongly, albeit subtly, think about whether you want it consciously or not.

Later you hear that you've not been selected for the job. Let's dissect what was happening energetically:

1) You're unsure if you'll be able to get on with colleagues (energy)
2) You see yourself fighting for recognition. In other words, you doubt your ability to be seen or get noticed. (energy)
3) Other negative thoughts have crept into your mind and strengthened your limiting beliefs (thought and energy)

If you want to take control of your life, then you must direct your thoughts to work positively so that it grasps the positive potential that is available. To get what you want in life, you must learn to picture the most ideal situation even in your hardest of times. Challenges will always be a part of life, but you can still accomplish a positive outcome through the potential you place in The Unseen. If you see yourself with challenges then simply imagine the ability to overcome them.

Influencing The Unseen effectively, means allowing yourself to dream, think and envisage possibilities which you may not have in your physical reality at the time. It's about creating, through the power of mind, intention and picturing the ideal life you want to lead. It is not helpful to focus on the life or reality that you're afraid of, this will only draw this closer to you.

Tools

Here are a few tips on using Faith to co-create and manifest your desires, and influencing The Unseen.

1- Start with thinking about something you know is going to happen soon. It could be an interview, an exam, a meeting with a client or any other event. Don't start with a dream that you want to happen in a year's time just yet, we'll come to that later in the book. I ask you to start with something in the nearby future because it's close to your thoughts and feelings now, and you're not likely to be distracted.

2 - If you already meditate, then take the event that is about to take place, into your meditation with you. If you don't meditate or find it hard to meditate, then day-dreaming works just as well. When you meditate or day-dream, let your mind wander to the event and play the event off in your mind as you would like it to happen. So, if it's an interview, then see yourself talking to your new boss. See him or her already as your boss. See yourself having conversations, getting on, smiling, talking and in agreement. Dare to see your boss congratulate you on your previous work. See them complimenting you on a skill or the experience you have. You can download a free meditation specifically for this via http://www.theunseen.net/free

In this process, it's important that you don't start doubting if the boss will you give you that compliment. You might start to think the compliment to be unrealistic or unlikely. When you do this, this contradicts the vision you're creating and this contradictory feeling (energy) gets sent out to The Unseen as a potential possibility. If you do discover some doubts, don't repress them, don't be afraid of them, just recognize them and correct yourself. Literally say, "Oh, I actually meant …" and carry on with your meditation or day-dream. This will eventually lead you back to feeling and envisioning good things.

3 - While meditating or day-dreaming, notice how you feel, but free yourself from judgment. Don't question why it feels good to idealize. It feels good because it is good and you don't have to question that any more. The questioning has more to do with the conditioning you have learnt. We all have the tendency to trust in the worst rather

than the best. It's a bad habit, but you're not alone in this. Trusting in yourself at this stage is very important, no matter how strange it may feel.

4 - Accept your feelings. It may feel wonderful, or if may make you feel scared. Accept this, this is normal. It's our resistance to new things and new ways of thinking that feels strange. It's not actually the event itself that causes these feelings. Remember this! You will feel out of place only because this is a new experience to you. It will bring up doubts because of our natural resistance. Ignore the voice of fear in your head. Keep at it and your feelings towards this will soon change.

5 - Find a moment every day, even if it's just 5 minutes, to day-dream or meditate about the event to come. Do exactly as explained in point 2. The best time of the day for day-dreaming or meditation is in the morning when getting started. After a good night's sleep our minds are open and relaxed and more able to take in new concepts. As you progress, start to meditate before you go to sleep as well. By meditating, positively dwelling or day-dreaming about this event in the evening, we emit our thoughts through our feelings, to The Unseen. When we fall asleep on these thoughts, our subconscious mind takes over and gives it even more power.

I'm going to leave you with one affirmation directly related to this principle of having faith in positive experiences. Read it as often as you like. Smile when you read it and let yourself be absorbed into its meaning. Think and feel deeply about what it would be like to really have faith in The Unseen.

Affirmation

I have faith in The Unseen because I AM the creator of my life.

❧ Chapter 2 ☙
Happiness From This Moment On

Introduction

Once upon a time, in a faraway land, there dwelled a village with a secret name. Everyone aspired to live there. That village was the place where all dreams come true, a village where complete and utter peace reigned and where calm existed as the norm. The village was a place where stresses were banished and where everyone lived together in perfect harmony.

It is a place that still exists today. It's the place that children can find the easiest, but lose as they mature. It's the place where one can escape all earthly problems and where fears and insecurities do not exist. Although this village is accessible for adults, many never seem to make it there. Their dreams of attaining residency are constantly pushed away. The more adults aspire to reach it, the more difficult it appears to get to.

From a distance, the residents of this village live wonderful, blissful and abundant lives. For those that aspire to be there, it looked as if the village residents have all they could ever dream of. It is true that those who reached the village understand the meaning of life, success and inner bliss, and have all they could dream of. What the village residents also come to understand was that before actually getting to the village, that the village was always much closer than they had ever imagined.

Explanation

This may sound like a fairytale, or perhaps something from Paulo Coelho's book, The Alchemist. The village is a metaphor for 'happiness'. It is indeed the place we all aspire to be and the feeling we desire to have. But it's also the place and space which we often postpone reaching. Happiness is experiencing no stress and no struggles together with the reality of feeling complete and utter bliss.

We have the tendency to say to ourselves, "If I have this", or "If I have that, then I will be happy". "If I just finish this project", "If I save enough money", "If I get good grades for my exams, then I can be happy". In this way, happiness is conditional. Through this type of thinking, we tell ourselves that in order for us to experience happiness, there must always be events, circumstances or conditions attached to it before it can become a part of our reality.

Is happiness then dependent on having things? And if so, will we then lose the experience of happiness once we lose the conditions attached to them? This is the psychological story we tell ourselves. In truth, we have been deluding ourselves. Happiness isn't attached to objects, people or conditions.

Happiness exists in the mind and is always available to us, even in our dreariest of moments. Happiness isn't a final destination by any means. You don't need to 'get' happy. You are happy or you are not, but it is you who decides.

Happiness is in fact a positive illusion and one that we can choose to create by the power present in our minds. It's the second principle of life with The Unseen. By allowing yourself to experience happiness in its own right, you can gain more of it. The old adage rings true: like attracts like.

So how do we do this?
You may have heard it before, but you must understand that happiness is experienced only in the present moment. You cannot experience happiness in the past or in the future. These moments do not exist. However, we can trigger present-happiness through thoughts about the past and future. Here are a few examples of how we experience happiness as a non-present concept:

1) Gratitude.
Note that it is used in past tense. You are grateful for something that you have already received or experienced. When you are feeling great, in the present time, you are simply experiencing happiness. Gratitude is an emotional experience derived from events in the past.

2) Expectation.
When you expect something, you are expecting a future event. A

positive expectation can induce a feeling of happiness, but again this is a future projection which has not taken place yet. Experiencing happiness towards an event yet to come is great way of influencing The Unseen, but it is not a method of experiencing happiness now.

The experience of true happiness is in its most powerful state, the ability to experience it in your present moment. You don't ned to aspire to happiness. You can experience happiness now, at this very moment. We do not need to postpone happiness through expectation. It is always available to us when called upon.

Example

Why is all of this important? When you expect yourself to be happy, later on, say, after you get that bonus or after you've found the love of your life, you tell The Unseen that you can only be happy if there are conditions attached to your happiness. But wouldn't you much prefer to experience happiness without conditions? Wouldn't you prefer to experience happiness without needing a reason to feel happy?

The Unseen is unbiased. Being unbiased means:
- There are no taking sides
- There is no judgment as to right or wrong
- There are no societal or moral influences
- There are no cultural or religious pressures or dictations
- There is no interpretation

Whatever you think about the concept of happiness is what you shall experience.

Scenario

Let's roll things around a little. We can experience happiness at any given moment when we drop our ideas of attachment and conditions needed to experience it. But happiness can only exist in the now. For example, as I sit in this chair, I feel the warmth from the sun through the windows. It makes me feel good now. Therefore, I am happy.

When I think of where my children are, I know they are safe at school and enjoying themselves. Therefore I am happy and I experience gratitude. I experience challenges, but I would only have these if I could handle them. Therefore I am happy, grateful and look forward (expectation) to what life will bring me. I could go on and on and on but at the end of the day, all I can confirm is that I am happy and I experience happiness through different perspectives – past, present and future.

If we want to focus on the happiness that is around us in the present moment, then all we need to do is focus on that which is available to us, at that very moment. It's easy to do. So let's try:

"As I sit in this chair, I feel good. I am healthy and alive. The room that I am sitting in has glass sliding doors that reveal a peaceful canal of flowing water. If I look outside, I see cloud scorched skies of white and blue. The light makes me peaceful and I am at one with The Unseen".

It's sometimes as simple as looking around, to experience what you have in front of you, that offers enough evidence of what you currently have to experience happiness in the present about. When you notice your happiness, The Unseen responds by giving you more happiness to experience. The feeling of Happiness is an energy which transmits at a high frequency. All thought and feeling energy is emitted at a certain frequency level because thought and feeling energy are waveforms and all waveforms have a frequency. A frequency is the rate in which the waveform moves. The higher the frequency, the happier you feel. The lower the thought or feeling, the slower the waveform moves and the more depressed or down you will feel. You know how heavy you feel when you have received bad news? This heaviness is what it feels like when your energy transmits at a low and slow rate. You literally feel your energy and your mood slow down. When someone says that they are feeling energetic, they are in fact experiencing a high frequency of energy within their bodies.

Thoughts and feelings of happiness raises our energetic vibrations and sends this energy out into The Unseen where all potential and all possibilities exist. To experience happiness from this moment on and through this moment, we need only look at what we have and be happy about it. The Unseen responds by providing more situations and events to help us thrive on that vibration. In any given moment, you need to choose happiness to have The Unseen respond with more happy experiences.

Tools

Here are a few tools to choose happiness in the present:

1) Learn to trigger Happiness. Happiness is an illusion of the mind that triggers a physiological and emotional response in our bodies (we feel good). You can trigger it at any time you like. So look at your life right now and choose to experience the things that are good. Not everything may be good, not everything has to be. Contrast forces us to be aware of what we do and do not have. It gives us the perspective to start choosing our own destiny. We can appreciate the contrast but at the same time, we can choose to see the things that make us happy now too.

2) Don't confuse gratitude for present happiness. Gratitude exists in the past and, although it makes us feel good to think about those things, it keeps us away from experiencing the happiness right in front of our noses. If you love to think of great events from the past try to bring it as much as possible into your current feeling now. Relate it to something that you are experiencing in your life right now. There is a thin line between gratitude and nostalgia and you want to make sure you stay on the gratitude end of the stream when recollecting the past.

3) Focus on what feels good. Expectation does wonders for The Unseen, but feeling good now is more important. Thinking of the future has a way of keeping us from the present. Life is created and continues to exist in your present moment. It is in the present that everything is manifested into physical reality.

4) Happiness is a choice. You may experience it on demand. The Unseen is there to provide you with all that you can imagine. Anything that you can think of and emotionalize can manifest. Before The Unseen can present you with the physical reality you desire, it needs to know that you really do want happiness without conditions. The point to remember is that The Unseen works much like a mirror. It reflects back to you what you give out. You inner world is your outer world manifested.

5) Don't pretend. The Unseen knows your energy through your deeper thoughts and emotions. If you're not truly happy with your life, this means that you need to let go of the thoughts that are making you feel unhappy. We're not talking about denial of your feelings, we are talking about not allowing negative thoughts and feelings to dominate your life. You can experience a challenge, feel bad about it, let it rest and then think of other things that make you happy. There are no rules that say you must experience disappointment for the rest of your life.

You can let go of grief with love and respect and move onto happiness whenever you allow yourself to. Being true to yourself is allowing yourself to experience the thoughts that you have and the feelings that come with it, but it's also allowing yourself to experience happiness whenever you want. The grief you may experience does not demand showering its darkness on all areas of your life. The grief you experience is an isolated energy resonating from an isolated event. You can have it there while at the same time experience joy for something else.

6) Don't be afraid of being happy even when you believe things are going badly. Remember, everything you see and experience around you is an illusion of your mind fueled by conditioning, past experiences, thoughts of yourself and ideas taken on from others. Once you shift your thoughts, then your feelings and emotions will change and The Unseen will create a new physical reality that reflects that . You are thinking not only for today, but also for all of your tomorrows.

Affirmation

I allow myself to be happy and I experience happiness at any moment I choose.

☙ Chapter 3 ❧
Manifesting And Deliberate Creation

Introduction

We often dream of a better life. A life where we have all of the things we need: a beautiful home, a nice car, perfect health and the love of our lives to share it with. In this dream, our life is perfect and all of our pains, fears and anguishes are no more. Suddenly, we are interrupted by the conditioned thought of this wonderful utopia being nothing but a silly dream...

We have an amazing ability to create just about any thought imaginable. Unfortunately, we're often better at destroying those thoughts through our innate ability to doubt and critique ourselves. Yes, we are very skilled in thinking of all of the worst possible things that could happen and we'll easily justify them by thinking of reasons, excuses and scenarios that 'could' pop up and take our dreams away. This is how we manifest these days. We justify our feelings by convincing ourselves to not even bother. The justification happens so quickly, that most aren't even aware of it happening. It's destructive and if we continue to approach our desires like this, then it may be better to not even dream at all. By imagining disastrous scenes in our minds eye, we fuel that potential within The Unseen. The disastrous scenes become reality. The Unseen is unbiased. It gives us everything we deeply think and feel about. As you wish, so is its command...

Explanation

Let's stop this way of thinking and try to get a better understanding of how we really can manifest the dreams we have into our physical lives. One mistake many of us make is thinking that The Unseen, via the Law of Attraction, works with all of our thoughts. This is not the case. If it were the case, then every thought we had would be manifested in our lives. The Unseen works only with certain thoughts that are charged with a certain energy. That energy is energy which exists within The Unseen. If a thought is created in our minds without the corresponding feeling to match it, it cannot be manifested. This is the reason why positive thinking, without positive feelings, doesn't work. A positive thought will always lead to a positive feeling. When this happens, we have a perfect match. When it doesn't, well, then we have a contradiction, which we'll go into a little more detail about later in the tools section of this chapter.

It's important to also understand that our conscious thoughts are not the thoughts that influence The Unseen at all. It is our subconscious thoughts that have power. The thoughts which are subtle and often unnoticed. The subconscious thoughts we have are the thoughts that come up in our heads in between doing and thinking other things. It's the thoughts that lie so deep that they are barely perceptible. It's the flash thoughts. The split second thoughts that leave almost as fast as they appear. These thoughts can come up in moments of inspiration (intuition) or moments of fear (ego). You'll be able to latch onto these thought more with practice, but the first requirement is to notice when you have them. Once you recognize them, you will be able to either stop them in their tracks or give more life to them if they offer you benefit.

We can start to distinguish our subconscious thoughts from our conscious thoughts by slowing down and being mindful of the responses we have every day situations. A lot of the time, our response to events is automatic. We give ourselves very little time to think and listen to our true answer. From the moment we are offered a cup of coffee in the morning to the first question we are asked at our work - our responses are mostly out of habit and rarely out of heart. If we would just take an extra 5 seconds to let the subconscious thought arise from beneath the habitual thought, we could allow our true selves to shine.

Our subconscious thoughts are powered and energized. These are our true thoughts and core beliefs. Once we are aware and ready to acknowledge their power, we bring ourselves closer to the potential available to us in The Unseen, and become receptive to the possibilities of manifesting and deliberate creation.

Example

The art of manifesting is much like any of the principles that affect The Unseen. We manifest constantly through our thoughts and the primary feelings we have about the smaller and bigger things in life. As the thoughts roll through our minds, we are constantly creating new moments in our lives. We need to start doing this process consciously, so that we get the things we really desire and deserve.

Manifesting is something that we do in the here and now. You may think that to manifest events into your life, you must think about the things you want in the future. For example, you have a car and you'd like a new one. What normally happens when manifesting, is that we think about the new car as a future reality- something that is not occurring now- but something we want to occur later. With this way of thinking your focus is on the future, in a linear time-line fashion and in a structured order, similar to that of the alphabet, A-B-C. As long as you see life occurring in a specific order, then you are experiencing life, based on the cause and effect theory. In other words, life remains a 'physical-first- time-line' of 'what you see is what you get'. This way of thinking means that you can only believe something is real if it is already in front of you.

So, what would happen if you discovered that life doesn't manifest in this way? What if life could manifest in a different order? What if you had to see with your mind's eye, experience with you heart and feelings, that what you desire, BEFORE it could be a physical manifestation in your life?

Let us zoom in on this for better understanding. If we think in an A-B-C style of structure, we will assume, in the example of getting a new car, that we first have to find a car (Step A). Next, we'd need to look at getting funds for the car (Step B) and the final step will be going to the dealer and finally making the purchase (Step C). In this example, we have a lot of conditions that will determine whether we can get that car or not.

The Unseen does not work with such chronological order. It does not need to materialize in sequences we are accustomed to. It does not need to take the A to B to C route, especially when it knows how to manifest things much faster and more efficiently than we can think of. If we turn the order around and not rely on the Newtonian method of acquiring things (ABC and Cause and effect), but instead, use the potential available in The Unseen, we're most likely to be offered a shorter route which would look like this:

1 - Manifest the car through the power of subconscious thoughts and intent, by simply seeing the car as a physical presence in our lives right at this moment (Step C)

And

2 - Await the possibilities from The Unseen to purchase or receive the car (Step B).

Scenario
When you imagine an event you'd like to happen in the future, The Unseen sees no reason to bring it into your reality quickly. Why would it? You've put it in the future. If anything at all, The Unseen will bring the physical manifestation of your thought/feeling energy at a later date. By imagining events to happen in the future, you simply delay its manifestation now. There's something else that also occurs when trying to manifest future events. Images of future events hold conditions to them. At a very deep, underlying level of your thought energy, you most likely see the event happening after another known event has preceded. This often happens when we are using our conscious thoughts to manifest. For example, you want a new car and you have a bonus or new job coming up. Even though the bonus or new job is not top of mind, it does have an energy you carry about with you already. What we tend to do in this example, is unconsciously link the bonus or new job to the arrival of the new car. The bonus/new job comes first and then we can justify the new car. It's the cause and effect theory all over again. This is not

manifestation. The art of manifestation and deliberate creation is the ability to experience the new car as if it is already on your parking spot, outside of your house, at this very moment, without a clue of knowing how it will get there, and free of conditions.

Society tell us that going from A to B to C is the logical order of events but The Unseen works very differently. The Unseen works only with the present to manifest energy into physical matter.

The "present" component in manifestation is supported scientifically by something called Quantum Entanglement. Quantum Entanglement was discovered in the 1930's by a collective of scientists that included Einstein, Bohr, Rosen, and Podolsky. and later through more research by Erwin Schrödinger. Simply said, Quantum Entanglement is the potential for a particle (matter) to appear in two places at the same time. We're not talking about two different particles, we're talking about the exact one particle being in two places at the same time, regardless of time. Those two places don't even have to be at the same point in time. They could both appear in the present as well as the future **AT THE SAME TIME**. This is vital to understand because it means that something could exist both as a particle and as energy - The car (particle) at your front door in the future and your thoughts and feelings in the present (energy).

The Unseen knows quantum entanglement like a brother. The Unseen operates on both spiritual (energetic) and scientific planes (particles). Time has no meaning within The Unseen. In other words, what you think and feel about today will not only influence your future, but also your past. Time-lines as we understand them, do not exist within The Unseen and this is fundamental in how you attempt to manifest your physical reality.

Think about the word and the literal definition of 'manifestation'. A manifestation is an event which takes place. It doesn't say an event which has taken place, nor an event that will take place. So, in other words, manifestation is something that can only occur in the now. Don't confuse manifesting with the material creation of that thing you desire. The word for that is realization. When that car or other object you want is in front of your nose, then the manifesting is over because it's a physical object in front of you. It has been materialized. So you must understand that manifesting can only occur in the present moment. It's what you do with your thoughts and feelings at each and every moment that governs what you are manifesting in your life.

Tools
Here are some tools and tips to help you manifest and deliberately create your own reality.

1 - Manifesting exists ONLY in the now. Time plays no role. Time is simply a reference we've conditioned ourselves to use, to allocate one moment to the next. Remember, time doesn't exist within The Unseen. It doesn't need it. If you want a good yet simple experience of the unimportance of time, just watch your pets relaxed at home.

2 - How to manifest correctly using the present time? If the only thing you have is now, this moment, then that means you already have everything you need or ever will need. Why? Because only the now exists, and if only the now exists, why do you push your dreams to tomorrow or the future? Again, you can and will convince yourself, or rather, justify your reasoning, but that just pushes you further away from what is happening now and manifesting now for you.

3 - Your task is to manifest everything into your life at this given moment. Manifesting is not the want of things to come, but the want to experience wholeness and abundance in the present.

4 - Could the real reason why you aren't getting the things you want in life be because you don't really want them? Or could it be because you simply don't believe it to be possible? In either case, you are right.

5 - Ask yourself these two questions: Do I really want to manifest good things into my life? Do I secretly fear good things won't happen, no matter how I much I want it? You need to allow good things to happen. You need to believe in them and permit them if you are going to manifest them.

Perhaps you don't think yourself worthy of it? If this is the case, then you must realize just how worthy you really are. We all have the same birthright. It's what you allow yourself to experience that counts. If you answered yes to these questions, then there's a good chance you have some subconscious limiting beliefs lurking deep inside that you have stronger feelings towards. Earlier in this chapter, I wrote about having a positive thought without a positive feeling and how this would result in a contradiction. If an contradiction occurs, this happens because you may have deep subconscious thoughts and feelings that have a much stronger energy than you other thoughts. It is certainly possible to think and truly believe in one thought whilst truly believing in its exact contradiction. This is also called cognitive dissonance which is

"[...] is the mental stress or discomfort experienced by an individual who holds two or more contradictory beliefs, ideas, or values at the same time, performs an action that is contradictory to one or more beliefs, ideas or values, or is confronted by new information that conflicts with existing beliefs, ideas, or values".

This very definition explains how important it is to be sure of what your true subconscious thoughts are whenever possible.

6 - Manifesting is experiencing the things you desire right at this moment, as if you already have it. Only then are you in the now and connected to The Unseen to realize your dreams. Can you practice imagining and believing that your new car is already sitting outside? It can be something else, of course. A new job, a lighter weight or anything you'd like to have or create. You can even manifest a new partner. The only thing you have to do is emotionalize the thought of having that thing you desire into your life as if it were happening now.

Affirmation
I have everything I need and everything I want.

❧ Chapter 4 ❧
Fake It 'Till You Make It

Introduction

Everything we see around us is simply a figment of the imagination. Our thoughts contain a web of images and feelings mixed in with emotions and associations (beliefs). Our version of physical life comes from the things we have learned through our upbringing. Our parents, schools, society and conditioning all influence our perspective on life and therefore what we see in the physical world. Everything we see and everything we experience is subject to what we have been taught to believe is true. If our lives and the objects, possessions and experiences are partly created through perception, then they are also subject to change, improvement, growth or decline, depending on how we look at things. It's the reason why, for example, that two people can have completely different experiences of an exact same event.

If everything in our physical surroundings is witnessed through perspective, then it must be possible that everything we observe and experience is interchangeable. By creating different thoughts and feeling towards what we see in our lives, we are able to create new realities. In other words, when we want to create something new, we must allow ourselves the ability to create a new version of an existing script.

We've all heard of the saying "Fake it 'till you make it". Faking the experience of things is what we do when we want to create new realities. The ability to use our imaginations to create (fake) something visually, in our minds and emotionally in our hearts, is the source of deliberate creation.

Explanation

The idea of faking something seems like a lie. The word 'fake' brings connotations in our mind of something being un-real or perhaps even untruthful. But what you should realize is that firstly, nothing is truly real, at least, there is not one version of an event. For example, what you experience after getting into a fight is a real and truthful experience to you. The same applies to another person on the other side of that same fight. That person may witness something else about the fight and have a different experience of it. Which is then true- his or yours?

Thoughts and emotions combined are what influences The Unseen and enables physical realities to manifest. If you can't 'fake' a vision, emotion or thought of the life you wish to lead, then you'll never be able to experience its physical counterpart. The old motto "ask, believe, and receive" rings true here. Asking is being clear on what you want. Believing means having faith that you shall get what you desire. Receiving means allowing the realization to occur in its own way.

Example

Let me give you a personal experience of my own. About three years before writing this book, I spoke with a friend about my business. The friend was eager to learn and interested in starting his own business. At the time my business was beginning to grow. In my mind the potential for further growth was inevitable. I saw my business at the beginning of a steep growth curve with much potential. I simply had good feelings about what the future would bring.

At one point, the friend asked me what my revenue was on a monthly basis. I replied by saying some months the revenue was a few thousand, and some months tens of thousands. That friend was impressed. In 'truth' the revenue was much less than the tens of thousands. After that conversation, I held on to the reality in my thoughts that my business would have varying revenue amounts of between a few to tens of thousands per month. In retrospect, I was 'faking' it. However, within a short time, I did see the revenue amounts climb. One month would show a few thousand and the next a doubling. This kept happening and at one point I suddenly saw the tens of thousands on the invoices we sent to clients, not once, but several times. I had faked this reality by simply allowing this potential to exist in my mind. I lived from that day on with an unwavering sense of confidence that this was how my business would continue. With that confidence, I infused myself with the associated feelings, emotions and experiences that would come with living an abundant life.

One of the things I wanted to do during that period was to travel. Together with my partner, Jeroen, we made the pact to travel every month. It became a game. One month Jeroen would choose a city/country and the next month I would. This made it fun and added a sense of adventure to it. In that year we visited a total of 9 different countries. By imagining, through the sheer power of the mind and the ideals of faith, together with setting a clear intention, we created the life we wanted financially and manifested the international travel we intended.

Scenario

Let's make it simple. Every time you take a vacation, you actually fake the entire process and this is what brings it to fruition. It may not seem like faking it, but what you do when planning a holiday is make the intention to go somewhere. At first, you see yourself on a pleasant beach in a warm and sunny climate. Next you see yourself reading a book in your sun chair with delicious cocktails next to you. Perhaps your ideal holiday is something completely different, but the process is the same. Before you can do anything, the possibility and vision must first exist in your mind. Even though vacations may seem like something not manifested through The Unseen, because perhaps you have already saved money for it, the process remains unchanged. You have to be able to visualize where you want to go, what you want to do and how you want to feel, before it can materialize.

This is a simple scenario that most of us have experienced before. But faking it until you make it goes even further and is not limited to knowing that you'll be going abroad. Faking it is what we do to plant the seeds of **ALL** that we want in life. There is no limit to it. You need to fake the experience and feelings as well as imagine a new reality. Faking it 'till you make it is the ability to create a reality without knowing how you'll achieve it. The Unseen is the realm that works out how this will become your reality.

Allow us to touch on this thing called honesty. We live in a society, where we have learned that being honest is good and being dishonest is not. When some people use the Law of Attraction to influence The Unseen, they often get stuck here. Deep inside they hear their self-talk telling them that what they are doing - the faking - feels strange and unauthentic. It does then feel strange and they began to disconnect from this vital stage of development. We must remember that it is our thoughts that determine how we feel. We feel unauthentic because our thoughts bring up memories from the past where we were caught for being dishonest. We were all taught as children not to lie. Our emotions simply confirm our thoughts and the cycle begins again. More thoughts of dishonesty, of being caught, of being 'told-off' appear and the negative feeling of 'faking it' gets confirmed.

In this situation, we start to think that we're deceiving ourselves. Even the idea of telling others about our newfound 'way of doing things' would probably result in them laughing at us. The result is that we become unmotivated and disillusioned and the faking doesn't even get started.

Tools
In the remaining chapter, I will be giving you tools to help you feel easy about faking it and help you fake things into your life with confidence.

1 - Define what it is that you want and write it down in one sentence. Keep it simple by starting with just one thing that you want to manifest. Try to keep it general, for example more money, a different car, a new house, etc. Don't yet define the details. Those will distract your process or bring in thoughts of doubt. You can progress to details down the road.

2 - Make a pact with yourself, and only yourself, to fake things into your life. This is your life, not anyone else's. This life is your sole responsibility. You don't need to tell anyone. There is a high chance that their opinions of what you are doing, will feed doubt into your mind and take you off track. Stop looking towards other people for approval of the things you are doing or what you want to achieve. You won't find it there. Even if others do believe in you, you still have to do it yourself.

3 - Think differently about what is true. If you feel like you are deceiving yourself, then it's important to realize that this is the only way to create the life you desire. It's not deception, rather it's a positive illusion. It's also possible that, through your conditioning, you cannot accept this new information as being true. If you can't learn to accept that this new information is possible, then you will not be able to create a new reality. If you cannot ask for new experiences from your own mind, you will not be able to achieve them.

Did you know that athletes, when training for competition, visualize themselves running their championship races and winning? There have been many scientific tests done to measure what happens in the brains of these athletes during their training and visualization. In fact, research conducted by Dr. Denis Waitley, with the Visual Motor Rehearsal experiment, successfully proved that even when we are visualizing an event in our mind, our physical and mental response produces the same output as when we are performing the event in physical life. What we send out to The Unseen, through our minds (faking it) or through taking physical action, is exactly the same. If faking it 'till you make it works for an athlete, why wouldn't it work you?

4- Fake living in a beautiful house now, with only the things you have. We're using this example but it can be anything really. How do you do this? Like this:

i - Tidy up! If things are in a mess, then the mess needs to be cleaned so that you have a new experience of being at home. If you live in the mess, you energetically exude untidiness, disorganization, lack of clarity and chaos. This is energy which also get sent out into The Unseen and The Unseen sees this as potential for more disorder.

ii - Make your bed. Your bed is the place where you get the rest needed to perform your daily operations in a productive and efficient way. Sleeping well at night ensures you wake up feeling revitalized in the morning. The better you feel in the morning, the more likely you'll have a better day despite any challenges you meet. You don't have to buy anything new. Just straightening your sheets every day is enough. It's easy and takes few seconds. Open a window to air out your room, use extra pillows to decorate your bed and ensure that it's inviting every night.

iii - Wash and pack your dishes away, every day. Whether you have a dishwasher or not, your kitchen needs to be free from annoying distractions and clutter. The feeling of clutter can create un-ease. Home is your safe haven, the place where you can escape from the outside world and retreat into your own.

iv - Pay attention to your closet space. Don't just throw things in there. Fold items properly or hang them after every use. It takes less than a minute to do so. If your bedroom and closet area is a mess, you create subtle mental stress for yourself.

How can you manifest a beautiful home if you live in a pig sty? Remember, what is on the inside is what is created on the outside, in our lives.

I've taken this example, which may seem odd to you, but is very relevant. Our homes are our bases. If we feel bad within our homes, we feel bad about ourselves. How you respect your home is how you respect yourself, so making it a discipline to live in a healthy manner is the same as allowing great things to come to you.

How you live reflects what you allow yourself. No matter what kind of house you live in, you can make it a beautiful home by showing yourself respect for how you live. When you keep this up, after a short time, you will experience a different feeling about your home. You have now not only faked the experience of living in a big beautiful home, you've also partly created it.

Affirmation
My home is my base and brings me peace and relaxation whenever I need.

ଓଃ Chapter 5 ଚ୍ଚ
Reality Is An Illusion

Introduction

If everything we see is pure perception, then there can be no limits to what we create with our minds and how we affect our reality. Wouldn't it be better to create a reality that is wanted, rather than living life under the assumption that what you see is all there is? Must we live by default, or do we have a say in the matter? The idea of reality being an illusion sounds as if what we see isn't real. This is not the case. What we see with our physical eyes is very real – it's just that the things we see and experience, isn't all there is to see or experience.

We have chosen to see the things we see and we have chosen to experience the things we experience. This is not an easy concept to grasp but there is a flip side to it. By claiming our right to experience the kind of reality we desire, we provide ourselves with the opportunity to make our lives better. We can allow ourselves improved, more meaningful and happier realities.

Explanation

If you played the lottery and I told you that you were going to win, you probably wouldn't believe me. Your mind has told you hundreds, if not thousands of times, that the chances of winning are so small that you shouldn't bet on it. Ultimately, if you do play, you play without believing that you're going to win and with that belief, The Unseen delivers you this potential as your reality. Now, you may be thinking that you didn't win because there are so many people who play. Or perhaps you believe that other people have more luck than you.

Let's take a few steps back to understand what's really going on and what affects us in these types of situations. First of all, the reason why you played the lottery is because you actually would like to win a load of money (who wouldn't?). The contradiction is that you don't think you're going to win and so inevitably, you don't. The Unseen can only work with the potential and possibility you provide it with. This you provide through your subconscious thoughts and feelings. A contradiction in thoughts and feelings confuses the energy you send out. The Unseen works with the intrinsic thoughts and feeling you have. It is this level of thinking that carries the most potential and is the most energized. The Unseen cannot, and will not deliver you something that you yourself did not think, feel or imagine possible. You worries or fears are also energized but The Unseen does not know the difference between thoughts of worry and thoughts of joy and hope. It will give you whatever you deeply think and feel about because this is the potential (through thought) you have provided it with, be it subtle or intense.

Example

The thoughts we have about our lives therefore, determine what our reality will be. What you think about, you bring about. The Unseen will never give us anything we do not believe in. Never! That lottery ticket will continue to cash out to other people instead of you because you can't conceive of the idea that it could ever happen to you. The Unseen is the field that holds all possibilities and all potential and the Law of Attraction is what you use to communicate with it. It's not the Law of Attraction that provides you with what you desire, but rather, The Unseen.

Now, some of you may be saying, or thinking in defense, that starving children would never ask for the situation they live in. This is another discussion all together, which I have written a number of articles about in the past. But let me tell you this, first. Do not use the example of starving children, poverty or other man-made nightmares to justify why The Unseen and the Law of Attraction can't exist or does not work. Thinking in this way is simply looking for reasons to justify why the Law of Attraction doesn't work. It's part of our human conditioning to look for proof, justifications and reasons to support our point of view. It's pointless trying to change the subject or divert the discussion. That doesn't change what is being said here. That will not change the way The Unseen works, whether you believe it or not. What we fail to accept is that, although our universe is a kind a loving place to be, the free will we have makes us the creators of our lives and of those around us. When we think about starving children in the world, we have to remember that the universe did not create this. We did. You did. I did. Together, collectively and with the rest of the people in this world, we are responsible. We may not have done it personally, but as humans, we have created poverty, destruction, wars and all of the hardships people suffer from. It is therefore our responsibility to fix it. The Unseen allows for this potential just as much as it allows the potential for you to win the lottery.

Scenario
Going back to the lottery scene - I play the lottery and I win at least 50% of the time. Sounds strange perhaps, but it's not really. You see, I believe I am going to win. It is my reality not because it happened before, although this certainly helps, but more so because, I think and feel I'll win. Whenever I buy a ticket, I am very hopeful and happy but afterwards, I just accept, welcome and allow the win to come. I don't even think about it consciously but subconsciously, my deep belief impresses The Unseen. It's possible for anyone to win, as long as you play and as long as you don't let limiting beliefs, such as the idea of not winning or of others being luckier than you, get in the way. I have won different amounts varying from a few thousand to several thousand Euros but also free things, including trips away, free dinners and more.

It's not a question of luck. Luck does not exist. I am not a particularly lucky person. No one is luckier than any other person. The difference is that I can visualize myself winning and I have a strong belief. Those of you who think others are luckier than you are, will always be unlucky. That's the perspective you've chosen and that will then be your reality. Reality is an illusion because the reality you experience is based on your perception of life around you. This includes everything from your personal relationships and how people respond to you, to how money flows to and away from you. It's all an illusion – the illusion you have created and the illusion you believe in.

Tools
Here are my tips and tools to help you with choosing your own reality

1 - Go into every situation in life knowing that the outcome will always be positive. You must rid your mind of negative ideas, especially those based on fear, or even worse, unfounded. Fear is not an excuse. It's a deadweight that brings you nothing. Even if your past experience of an event has been negative you must realize that the past is really no reflection of the future, unless you make it so. You make it so by thinking you know what reality is, how it operates and thinking that what you see is all there is. You make it so by creating images in your mind of what the past looked like and assume that will be your future also. Reality is what you think and feel it is. As the saying goes, "Watch what you ask for. You just might get it".

2 - There is no such thing as luck. Period! Stop using this as an excuse to not change your perception or see other perspectives. Thinking that others are luckier than you are holds you in stagnation. You will never be able to move forward if you are constantly affirming this. Letting go of this idea means making a change in yourself about how life is. It also means taking responsibility of how you want your life to be from this moment on.

3 - Stop being afraid of doing things wrong and making mistakes. We are perfectly imperfect humans destined to make mistakes but also destined to have huge successes. Mistakes are not indicators of a lack of success. It has nothing to do with it. We learn through our mistakes. We gain new insights, perhaps certain insights which we may not have received had we not made those mistakes. So, allow yourself to make the mistakes but learn to isolate the idea of limitations as a result of your mistakes. Whatever you may have done, right or wrong, good or bad is always contained within an isolated event. The version you see in your mind's eye must be the improved version if you want a different outcome in your reality.

4 - Understand that reality is not the objects or possessions in your life. Your life is what you have created. Reality does not create your life. It's the other way round. Your thoughts affect your feelings and your feelings send signals out into The Unseen through the Law of Attraction. Creating the reality you want means taking responsibility and taking the power which is inherently yours. Everything around you is an illusion. Choose the illusion that benefits you the most. It's yours for the taking.

Affirmations
I choose the reality that benefits me most.

CB

The thoughts we have about our lives determine what our reality will be. The Unseen will never give us anything we do not believe in. Never!

ও Chapter 6 ৯০
Universal Secrets

Introduction

What would you do if you could have anything you wanted? How would you feel if there were never any shortages? What would your life look like? These are questions we rarely ask ourselves. We rarely dream of our most ideal situation. We don't dare to. We're too afraid of it not materializing. We're too afraid of being disappointed. We're too afraid of being hurt and so, we forfeit the dream. We forget about it and tell ourselves that our desires won't come true and that life just doesn't work that way...

If I told you, that you and I, your mother, brother, your sister, neighbor or best friend could have everything and anything they wanted, would you want to believe me? I didn't ask if you believed me. Did you notice? I asked if you'd wanted to believe me. Like most people, we all want the best for ourselves and in the ideal world we would easily answer with a straight forward and wholehearted YES. But for now, let's go back to the specific question of whether you would want to believe me. I think the answer is yes, and I understand and perhaps even feel your hesitation at the sheer thought of the question and your answer. Despite wanting this, you, deep within, most likely felt some resistance to answering the question. What you felt was the ego's attempt to protect you. It said, "Don't go there, you're only going to get yourself hurt". It called up subconscious memories and thoughts from the past. Doubts which you may not even know you had. How do I know this? I know this because this amazing universe of ours is one and we are all connected through time and space. I know this because it is a limiting belief that most of the world's population shares. Collectively, we have learnt to protect ourselves by limiting our scope of possibilities. By limiting the idea that more could be possible for us, we prevent ourselves from getting hurt, should it not work out... at least, that's what our ego tells us. The universe however, feels differently about this. The universe can only express itself through us and so by denying your own light, you too deny the universe and everything contained within it, the very same thing.

Explanation

We are one. You and I are connected to each other energetically. A type of telepathy perhaps. In fact it is through telepathy that clairvoyants and psychics can do their work. They are simply able to tune into thought energy waves, all of which are present in The Unseen and available to all of us. All thoughts and feelings of ourselves, our world and our potential, resides in The Unseen. All desires and doubts about the achievability of those desires, are also present in The Unseen.

When your desires vibrate at the same frequency as my desires, we are connected. This applies to every person on earth. When you have an idea – to start a new project or new activity, for example – you tap into The Unseen. Within The Unseen, the potential for your new idea or activity to manifest into physical form begins to take place- if you let it. You've probably experienced a situation before where you have ideas for something new, and then suddenly someone contacts you and enquires about that idea you had. Some people will write this off as coincidence, but within The Unseen, coincidence does not exist. Your idea is energy and this energy resonated with energy from someone else. For example, you have an idea to start a book keeping service whilst someone has the idea to start a business and needs book keeping services. This is a simple example of how different energies line up to each other within The Unseen.

We can look at our lives from a spiritual point of view and say that we are spiritual beings in a temporary human body, experiencing human life. We can also look at our lives and our existence from a scientific point of view, namely, the view point of quantum physics. Whichever perspective we choose to take, we still arrive at the exact same conclusion, namely, energies always align. To use coincidence as a form of reasoning, we give away our power and potential to control and contribute to the fulfillment of our lives. What power do you give yourself by saying that events are random? Randomness is pointless. Pointless circumstances which have no relation to anything.

Why would such an intelligent universe create circumstances without any purpose?

Example

Quantum physics is the law of potential and probability. In short, it states that anything and everything in this universe is possible, as long as that 'any-thing' can be imagined in our minds. Quantum physics states that, everything that exists in the imagination has the potential to exist in our physical world. It confirms that an energetic field is present throughout the universe and that this field is available to us all. It also states that we are a part of that field.

This field is where the physical creation of objects, events or experiences becomes tangible matter. Within this field lies only potential and probability, in the form of energy. For a physical manifestation to occur, the energy waves within The Unseen need to match other resonating energy waves. Thoughts have feelings and feelings are made up of energy waves. Thoughts tell us how to feel. If we think good thoughts, we will feel good feelings. The same applies to negative thoughts. These let us know that we should feel bad. Through our feelings, we have access to The Unseen. All feelings vibrate at a certain frequency and so, to create a physical manifestation from feeling energy, we simply need think of an event to come and project this into The Unseen. This is done subconsciously most of the time, but it is also possible to do this with intent – also known as, deliberate creation. Our thoughts create the mental images and our feelings send the energy associated with it. The blending of corresponding thought (images), and feelings (energy), then comes together in The Unseen. This results in physical manifestation.

There is no escaping The Unseen. We are all part of this field. When we tap into and access The Unseen, any thought, feeling and desire can be created. Through The Unseen, we can manifest everything that is in our hearts desire.

"Everything is energy and that's all there is to it. Match the frequency of the reality you want and you cannot help but get that reality. It can be no other way. This is not philosophy. This is physics." – Albert Einstein.

Science confirms that there exists a divine intelligence. Religions confirm the same and both science and religions tell more or less the same story. There are quotes from the religious books, such as the Bible "Ask and it shall be given you" Matthew 7:7-8 which is another way of saying 'Ask for what you want and trust that you will receive it'. The Torah says "One who trusts in God, kindness surrounds him!" and "Fortunate is the man who puts his trust in God!" Zohar II:184b. The meaning is then to place ones trust in God (The Unseen) and have faith that life will be surrounded by goodness. In the Quran the Prophet Mohammed even says "[…] Were he to ask something of Me, I would surely give it to him, and were he to ask Me for refuge, I would surely grant it." Again we see from the Bible, The Torah and the Quran similar messages being communicated. As old as these books are and whatever faith you may or may not have, the message is simple. To trust in The Unseen is to grant yourself access to all that is needed.

The Unseen works with faith but offers the possibility to give you want you want through the power of your thoughts and feelings. Without doubt, you shall receive that which you have asked for. Could the answer to life be as simple as having faith? Can we imagine allowing all that is possible into our lives through the power of intent and belief? It sounds so simple, and actually, it is.

Scenario

A few years ago, I was looking for an office for my business. I had made the intention that the office should have lots of windows and be bright with lots of light. I pictured arched doorways and lots of glass. I also envisioned that the office have enough space for my team. The office we were in at the time, was too small for my growing business.

One afternoon, while driving back from a meeting, I noticed a beautiful building located on the water side. On the outside of the

building was a huge poster. The poster read 'The Bell - Spaces Available". I'd driven past this spot many times earlier, but had never noticed this building before. The look of the building excited me. It had been completely refurbished and renovated, but the original design of the building was kept intact. I had never seen the building from the inside, so I was curious.
THE UNSEEN

When I got home that evening, I jumped straight on the computer and looked up the website to The Bell offices. I looked at the photos of the spaces available. It was exactly what we were looking for. The spaces were full of light with high ceilings, huge windows and even glass doors. I decided to call The Bell in the morning. Later that night, I went to bed, full of anticipation and thoughts that about The Bell. I was exhilarated, happy, excited and could hardly sleep. My whole being was consumed by the thought of being in this office.

The next day, after I arrived at my office, I told my colleagues about what I had seen. I showed them the website and the photos and they all looked on, eager and enthusiastic. We shared the dream of moving to this fantastic new office. All I had to do now was make the call. I picked up the phone, dialed the number on the website, and was greeted by the friendly receptionist on the other end. I explained that I had seen the poster on the building and that I was calling to enquire about the availability. She responded by saying that everything was full and that there was nothing available. A slight feeling of disappointment came over me. She then continued and said that I could call back in a few days' time to see if something had become available. I thanked her, ended the call and continued with my day. I couldn't stop thinking about that office. I saw images of the office and my team in there, the whole day through. I simply couldn't get it out of my mind.

A few days later, I decided to call again. I asked if there was space available. The receptionist replied with the same message - there was nothing available. She apologized. I said thank you and returned to my work. For some reason there was something in me that would not let go of the office. Despite the news she had given me, I still felt the need to keep at it. This time, however, I was much more relaxed. I decided to wait another two days and try again. Every moment I could, I would look at the photos of the website. I imagined us holding meetings with clients there. I imagined myself sitting in the large empty space and meditating there. I envisioned everything

possible and everything that made me feel good about being in that office.

Two days later, on a Friday afternoon, I decided to call one more time. The same receptionist answered the phone. I asked if there was office space available. For some reason, this time, I was expecting a different reply from her. I don't know why this was or what kind of answer to expect, I only knew it would be different, and it was. This time, the receptionist said that she would get someone to call me back shortly. I happily agreed, gave her my telephone number and hung up. Within an hour the phone rang. My colleague answered the phone and passed the receiver to me. A man's voice spoke and said "I understand you're interested in one of our offices. Well, I'm pleased to tell you that an office has just become available. Would you like to come and take a look?"

I literally jumped with joy. How can this be? I had called 3 times and each time there was nothing available. As kind as the receptionist was, she told me every single time that there were no spaces for us. Somehow I still believed without a shadow of a doubt, that there would be office space for us.

The next week, I took my team to see the office. We were all very excited. We stood in the spacious office looking and devising how we'd all fit in and where our desks would go. It was just perfect. Within weeks we were able to move into the office with high ceilings, large windows and huge amounts of light. It was a space with an open floor plan, perfect for my collaborative group. This manifestation was created simply by the power of intention. Our physical realities are not all that there is. I could have accepted the kind receptionist telling me there was nothing available, and left it at that, but I realized that what we see, hear and experience is not all truth. My thought and feeling energy had met its match in that space becoming available. The wave collapsed and became physical matter. It was at this moment that I really understood how our The Unseen works within the universe.

Tools
Here are some tips and tools in working with the energetic connections in the Universe.

1 – Make your desires clear. You have to know what you want in order to receive it. What we often do when we want something badly, is think of the thing we want and then think of the things that might cause it to not happen. This is natural, but it's a bad habit too. The Unseen is a loving, caring, and giving field. It wants what you want just as badly as you do. Why do we then poison our own good intentions by thinking of negative scenarios? Why do we spoil it in this way? By making your desires clear and pure and without the what-if's, we send the energy of this desire into the field of The Unseen. The field then does whatever it must do to manifest it into physical reality. All we have to do is be very clear on what we want and not let any fears get in the way.

2 – Forget about how it will happen. You have no idea anyway. Our job is to focus on the desire and the intention and nothing else. We must realize that, although we are clear on what we want, we don't often know what the best way is to achieve it. We're control freaks at heart. We have learned to plan every step of our lives, even if it's been to our detriment. The Unseen knows the quickest and most efficient route to the manifestation of our desires. It is often in ways we could have never have thought of. Just like in my example, I kept persevering with the calls despite being told there was nothing available but it was The Unseen that worked its way through all the rejections and revealed how it manifests best. Let The Unseen do its works.

3 – Accept that you can have anything and everything you desire.
This is the hardest of all to accept because we've been told that in order to achieve anything in our lives, that life must be hard and difficult. This is the biggest amount of B.S. there is and we've accepted this belief because it's been said hundreds if not thousands of times to us throughout our lives. It is certainly not a fact. It's just what we've been conditioned to believe. Belief and expectation form realities. Let it at least be the belief and expectation that you want, rather than that which you do not. Change your thinking, allow the impossible to be possible in your mind, and allow yourself the abundance in which you are all entitled. It's all there in The Unseen and it's just as much yours as anyone else's.

Affirmation
Every desire is possible, pure potential.

⚃

Could the answer to life be as simple as having faith?
Can we imagine allowing all that is possible into our lives through
the power of intent and belief?

☙ Chapter 7 ❧
Design Your Life

Introduction

Everyone wants to lead a wonderful life. It's natural to want the very best of things and our loving, caring, compassionate universe wants the same thing for you too. *"What you seek, is seeking you"* – Rumi

As we are all connected to the universe, and we are each an individual expression of the universe, it seems only natural that we should want to grow and experience more and more. The universe needs growth. Growth is a form of evolution, change and magnanimity. As individual expressions of the universe, life edges us towards more experiences whereby we can become the best versions of ourselves. And in becoming the best versions of ourselves, we shine a light and become examples to others of how great they too can become.

Explanation

Creating the type of life we want is an active process. It doesn't just happen because we have free will. We have free will to do what we desire and that includes doing nothing at all. When we want to create a conscious life and live deliberately, we have to take active steps to achieve this. It encompasses everything from getting out of bed each morning to making major changes in our lives. Designing the life you want means thinking about what we want our lives to look like, moment-to-moment, day-to day and year-to-year. The idea of being able to scope our lives is what makes life fun and enjoyable. We get to choose.

Explanation

For some reason, we have told ourselves that, in order to get what we want, we must work hard. Again, this doesn't really make sense. If the universe is loving and caring and wants to give us what we want, why would the universe make it hard for us to achieve? Are these then the words of the universe or is this something we've been telling ourselves and passing down from generation to generation? How destructive we are being? Life isn't difficult, but life IS what we think it is. Life is what we make it. Our lives are a direct reflection of our thoughts and feelings. If we expect something to be difficult, then you can pretty much guarantee yourself that it will be just that. But this also applies to life being easy. Take any example. Think of something which you know will be easy to do or achieve. You'll probably be thinking that it was easy to do because you knew how to do it. But doesn't this apply to everything? Once we know how to do things, then those things we want to do become are easy, right? So, why not apply this to every single aspect of your life?

Example
Life is about perspectives and the perspectives we choose to live from. These perspectives are our own. When we actively decide which perspectives we want to live from, we design our lives and this is called Life Design. So, how have you designed your life? Have you chosen a life design full of hardships, or a Life Design full of ease?

Life design is the act of planning how you want to live your life. We all need to take an active part in this process. It's more advantageous to live the life you really want to live, than living a life by default.

Scenario
In 2008, I decided to create my Life Design. There were some essentials that I wanted in my life and so I wrote them down. I wanted to do whatever I wanted to do. This was the first thing on my list. Now, that may seem very broad, but I wanted it to be all encompassing. I wanted it to include freedom of choice, in everything from the food I ate, to the hours I worked. I wanted it to include being with my children when I wanted, or being able to take them to school or daycare when I wanted. I wanted it to include being able to see my family when I chose, to traveling when I wanted. Ultimately, my first Life Design choice was about freedom.

From this first option, I could fill in the blanks. The blanks were areas such as work, personal time, social time, family time and wealth, and these all relate back to the Law of Attraction, the universe and The Unseen. In order to create the life I wanted, I had to get clear on what I desired. I had to accept that all of these things were possible, even if I didn't know how to get them. If I focused too much on how to achieve all of these things, I would easily have thought of what things I needed to do to achieve them. Consequently, fear would have crept in, together with the, what if's and limiting thoughts, and destroyed my dreams long before they even had a chance to manifest.

Tools
Here are some tips and tools to live a life by design rather than default.

1 – Take a piece of paper and write down how your ideal life would look like. Make it as vast, broad and ideal as you want and don't be afraid to think big. This exercise is about getting clear on what you want. You have to dare to be bold otherwise you'll miss opportunities.

2 – Make it more specific. If you've written down that you'd like more free time, then write down in what way you'd like to have the free time. Would that be to do sports or to read? Or perhaps you want more time to cook or follow a course or hobby? It really doesn't matter what it is, as long as it's something you want. It can be anything you like or anything you'd really like to do for yourself. You're allowed, so take this step by getting it down onto paper.

3 - Get into detail and add another item to your list. Add items about money, travel, recreation, your home, your family, your work/business. Don't limit yourself now. How much would you like to earn, per month, per year, etc.? How often would you like to travel and to where? Write it down as if there is nothing to stop you. It may feel strange a first, almost as if you're kidding yourself, but you're not.

You're taking the well-needed time to define your life and plan it according to your specific desires and needs. You have to start somewhere otherwise you'll only be living unintentionally.

Affirmation
I love the life design I've created for myself.

ɞ

Our lives are a direct reflection of our thoughts and deep feelings. If we expect things to be difficult, then you can pretty much guarantee that life will be just that.

❧ Chapter 8 ☙
Success Is For Everyone

Introduction

There is this idea that many people have. They think that the universe operates with principles such as favoritism and discrimination, and that some people are simply luckier than others. The universe is a divine source of energy and intelligence. It is a living, breathing organism that fills the earth and everything, including ourselves, within it. It does not discriminate because it gains no advantage in doing so. Favoritism does not apply.

When we say things to ourselves, like, this or that person is lucky, we diminish our own power. By not recognizing the potential of life that is available to us, we limit our choices. By limiting our choices, we remove the options and possibilities that are inherent to us as individual expressions of the universe.

Explanation

The energy of the universe has no eyes to see, no ears to hear and no hands to feel. The only thing it is does have, is the ability to connect with our feelings, emotions and thoughts, and translate them into physical reality. In its highest form, this energy operates on varying frequencies and benefits most when we are able to align ourselves to high vibrating emotions such as love, peace, compassion, empathy, understanding, knowing, trust and faith.

As humans, we are raised to have limiting beliefs. These are beliefs we take on from our upbringing, but also from society in general. Collectively, we are taught that only few can be successful, and that abundance isn't for everyone. Instead of questioning if this is actually true, we take these ideas on and they become a fundamental part of our belief system. Our reality then begins to take shape and our ideas become manifested in the physical world. We see the proof of our thoughts reflected in our physical domain and so we believe that this is what life is all about.

We have convinced ourselves that what you see is what you get. Newtonian physics states that we live in a world of cause and effect. This logic is 150 years old. If we accept it at face value and do not account for the developments in science, and the deeper understanding of how the universe operates, then accepting new ways of thinking will be a challenge.

Example

The ability to experience success does not rely on any condition other than the notion that success is accessible for you. There are large groups of people in the world who feel that success is not an option for them. They can feel discriminated because of the color of their skin, their age, their education, status or other reason. Certain people within these groups will walk the earth with a constant feeling of being victimized, having less chances and generally feeling as if fewer opportunities are available to them. They have convinced themselves that success will never be their experience. They walk around with a self-imposed handicap under the illusion that their desires are at the control and mercy of other groups. They completely give away their power out of a lack of responsibility. The world around them naturally must confirm this. The proof they see manifests in anything from job application rejections, to be being refused a table at a fancy restaurant. Every rejection confirms this feeling and the energy perpetuates the next round of disappointments in the queue, ready to appear.

Racism, discrimination and prejudice absolutely exist and they are very real effects of negative energy between individuals and groups. There are people on this earth who will use any means possible to make another feel less and inadequate. These people feel the need to walk through life expecting their achievements to be taken away from them, they're jobs given to other people and their safety endangered by cultures they are ignorant of. These people will always blame others for their failings. They'll say "they passed me over because of diversity". They will always have an excuse for the lack of direction they have in their lives. Their chances of success is always dependent on someone else. These people walk through life in fear, afraid their positions will be threatened and their statuses destroyed. They too see proof from the news in the media of terrorist attacks and assume that terrorism will soon be on their doorsteps. Their idea of liberty will soon be threatened and so, for them, the only way forward is to put others down in whichever way possible and generalize all. Little do they know however, that the sheer act of doing this simply creates the manifestation of negative events for themselves.

Both of these groups of people have something in common. The victims and the discriminators are not opposing each other but rather, aligning with each other. Their energies are in perfect resonance. What they fear is just as certain to turn up in their physical lives whether they are right or wrong.

Unconsciously, both have convinced themselves that their success is reliant on the eradication of the other. They are both as weak as each other, and both fueled with excuses and reasons for their lack of success and happiness. One cannot work with the positive potential of The Unseen if they do not see it, and one cannot benefit from it if they are convinced that others are masters of their destinies. The victims and the discriminators share the same negative concept of forcing their power or values onto those that try to oppose it. By confirming their fears in thought and strong feelings, both groups are blinded by their own negative illusions and locked into The Unseen potential of confines and restrictions.

Scenario

The Unseen does not care where you are from, what you have done, where you were born or what your place in society is. These are human specifications used to group and label each other. The Unseen does not provide any group or individual with any more success than the other. It just provides what has been energized through the Law of Attraction.

There is no monopoly on success. Success is attainable for everyone. Success is not a tangible object. Success is subject to interpretation. Success is a mindset. Success is the allowing of pleasurable things and experiences into our lives, regardless of what others think of you and most importantly- success for is each and every one of us, our birthright. The issue at hand is this…how much success do we individually and collectively allow ourselves? How far will you go to release any prejudices you may have in order to allow more success into your own life? How far will you go to shut out ideas of racism being the blockage in your life and how far will you go to admitting that your own fears are the very things preventing you from moving further? You are who you think you are. You experience the pleasures or the trials of what you think you are worth. No matter how you see this, or what your experiences have been, you are the master of your fate.

Success is energy, much like the energy of love. In order to feel love, we must tune into thoughts and feelings that make us feel love. The energy of success is the same and available in the field of The Unseen, to us all, as potential. If you are living your life with the idea that you cannot achieve success because of other people or other groups, then your reality will be just that. The Unseen will confirm to you that what you think. As you have asked it shall be given. To access the universal success available to us is simple. All we have to do is tap into it and allow it to come into our lives through the power of our thoughts. It could require a radical change in our ways of looking at life and the people within in. It will require us to make a paradigm shift and accept that we have been seeing things not as they are, but as we want them to be. We must not only think the truth of how things can be, we must also feel it. We must do what we can to imagine the idea of success, despite our circumstances. This means looking beyond what is in front of our physical eyes, however horrifying we experience it, and envisioning a complete opposite. This is how we tap into the experience of success and create the physical manifestation of it.

Tools
Here are some tools to illustrate how universal success is, and how likely you are to succeed in life.

1 - What is your idea of success? Write down what you think it would feel like to be successful. There is no right or wrong answer. Success is what you make it. Success is how you experience it. It's personal. If your ideas are negative, then write the opposite of the negative ideas in a column next to it. The positive ideas should now become your focus.

2 – Get to terms with the idea that luck doesn't exist. Until you realize that you are not unlucky in life, you will always struggle with the idea of success and this will block its flow to you. Only when you release your resistance to, and limiting beliefs about, success can you allow it to flow to you.

3 – Watch successful people, read their biographies and blogs and get inspired them. Use their stories as a motivation. They started out just like you. They had their fair share of challenges, but they knew success was possible for them simply because they saw themselves leading successful lives. They are really not different from anyone else. If it worked for them, why wouldn't it work for you?

4 – Release the limitations you place on yourself. If you feel discriminated, you will experience discrimination. Releasing the feeling of discrimination lies solely within yourself. It is your responsibility. If you first need others to prove to you that they are not discriminating, you will never be free of your need for their approval. This is not freedom. This is not what is meant for you. If you are the one discriminating, then you must come to terms with your own fear about yourself. Discrimination shows an aspect of insecurity. One discriminates against another out of competition or jealousy. If this is the case, then the question to ask yourself is what you fear losing or what you fear will be taken away from you. Being honest about this will help you to come to terms with it and eventually release the limitation you place on your chances of success.

Affirmation
I too, AM the energy of success.

ⳙ Chapter 9 ⳗ
Financial Attraction

Introduction

Haven't we all dreamt about being incredibly rich? What fun it would
be to be able to buy beautiful houses, cars, to go shopping, travel and
the works. Of course we have. We did this a lot as children. When we
were small, we could imagine a life of dreams and riches. We told
ourselves that we'd become lawyers, just like in the series LA Law,
or for today's generation, the series Suits. Perhaps we'd become
pilots and fly around the world or even actors, becoming a star and
live in Hollywood. How great it was to be a young child. How great it
was to aspire and what a pity that we don't dream as freely as we
used to. What a shame that we've become afraid of imagining a life
bigger than our current reality, and what a tragedy that we no longer
truly aspire to wealth and abundance.

Many of us have chosen the safe road. We tell ourselves to
hope for the best and expect the worst. Just read those words again
"hope for the best,... expect the worst" – yes, a very detrimental way
of thinking. We've come to use this type of thinking as a form of
protection. We use it to protect ourselves from disappointments and
failure. As a consequence, we block any chance of such wealth ever
coming to us.

Explanation

There is something that exists which is called a financial blueprint.
It's something we were not born with, but a thing which we all carry
around with us. It's a map of sorts, devised in our heads with outlines
of our financial possibilities. It contains our version of the concept
and importance of money; how we view it, how we've experience it,
how we value it and its meaning in our lives. As with everything in
the universe, our financial blueprint holds energy. That energy is
determined by our thoughts, feelings, emotions and our experiences
around money. This energy works like a magnet, either drawing us
towards or away from financial success.

In order to understand what kind of energy our financial
blueprint has, we need to be honest with ourselves about our feelings

towards the concept of money. This means delving deep into our past, our childhood, and looking back on the experiences we witnessed as children. Most people are brought up having bad experiences of money because they saw their parents having difficulty with it. We witnessed them struggle and because we were young and still developing, we internalized what we saw as being something we may have caused. Now, it's not quite as straight forward as this sounds but the internalization occurs when for example, we are with our parents in the supermarket and we ask for sweets or candy. Most often, our parents told us No. If we asked again, we'd get a harsher response and if we moaned, which we all did, we'd then get the answer that filled us with guilt. Our mother would respond by saying "No! We can't afford that" or "I don't have money for your silly sweets". The internalization begins through a series of negative emotions we experience from that event. By asking a question which resulted in our mothers getting upset with us, we experience guilt. We then feel bad for making our mothers feel bad and experience more guilt or even shame. In terms of finances, can you now see, from this simple example, how our relationship with money is beginning to form? Do you see the blueprint being made? As children we interpret our parents financial issues partly as being something we have caused (asking for that candy), but also as the things that cause (emotional) pain to them and later on to ourselves.

From a very young age, money has an important role in our lives and even power over the potential of our financial future. Our financial blueprint is therefore derived from childhood experiences which we take on into our own adult experiences. If our parents had enough money and your childhood experience is that there was always enough, then you'll likely to have a healthy financial blueprint. If however, your parents were affected by financial difficulties, then your blueprint will be tainted by the idea of shortage.

There is another aspect we must look at within this chapter and that is that of financial knowledge. Financial knowledge and experience is the one thing which doesn't mature by itself. As we mature, we grow and learn new ways of being, with ourselves or with people or situations around us. We become responsible, for example, or we become disciplined to get ourselves out of bed in the mornings. Strangely enough, this doesn't happen at the same rate with our financial knowledge. We don't suddenly learn how to save or pay our bills on-time, even though we know we should. Instead, we learn how to spend. We learn that money is freedom but we don't realize the deep spiritual hold money has on us from the past.

The shortage we experienced as children takes a strange turn the moment we start earning money for ourselves. What we couldn't have then, we can buy ourselves now. This all sounds good, but what also happens is that we encounter the same shortages as our parents did because this is what we saw happening when we were younger and so the cycle continues. Deep in our subconscious thoughts we truly believe that money is hard to come by and even harder to keep and this becomes our financial blueprint. Our financial blueprint is spiritual and tangible. A lack of financial knowledge both practically and energetically creates a narrow financial attraction.

We're either brought up with the idea, albeit subtly, that money is scarce or money is abundant. Without conscious knowledge of what our financial blueprint is, money will always be associated with the concept of scarcity and limitation. The financial knowledge we take into our lives as adults, is pretty much only what we get in school, but this does not teach us how to deal with our experience of money spiritually and so we are often unaware of what we are sending out about money into The Unseen.

Example
You cannot fix a problem unless you can see that a problem exists. Before progressing to the tools section of this book, let us first take

the time – as this is such an important aspect of our lives – to know what

our deep feelings are towards money. We can take an example by looking at a large bill which is due. Take a significant bill as an example. Everyone has bills to pay. Almost everyone has, more often than not, more bills to pay than our monthly income can cover. For the majority at large, their financial blueprint is one of lack rather than prosperity but even this can be changed and redirected into a positive financial blueprint.

Now, this little exercise is probably not going to draw great feelings within you, but that's the whole idea. In doing this exercise, what we're trying to do is understand what our relationship to money is. When I say relationship, I mean how we feel about the topic of money in our lives. When we're confronted with a large bill that needs to be paid, whether we have money in the bank or not, there will be an thought and an emotion connected to that confrontation. That thought or feeling can come up in a flash within you. It is likely to disappear very quickly too – that's our ego's way of not wanting to deal with the feelings associated with it. That thought will be one of two things: positive or negative, and the feeling will lay the basis of our relationship with the ebb and flow of money in our lives. This feeling is the energy contained within our financial blueprint and is what we need to understand more of, and get in touch with, in order to make changes and produce the financial abundance we seek.

Scenario

So, how does it feel to have to pay that large bill? Are you totally relaxed with it without any worries, or is there a slight sting in having to pay it? If you experienced the sting then this could be because paying bills, brings up annoying and possibly, painful memories from your childhood – like what you parents had. There's a paradox in their too, which we'll get to in a moment. Your parents experience is not your experience. This is the first thing you have to let go of. You are not experiencing your parents life. You can only be experiencing your own. What your parents experienced is no reflection of your own life. In fact, we often see children who were brought up in financial shortage, excel financially as adults. They have somehow taken their childhood experience and used that as a stepping stone in helping them achieve financial abundance.

The paradox in paying for the large bill, despite the feelings you have towards doing that, is being able to accept that spending money on anything and everything is a great opportunity when you enable yourself to change your perspective on it. Everyone loves spending money, it's just that we only like doing this when we can appreciate what we are spending our money on.

For example, most of us love spending money on ourselves. We also love spending money on our families and friends. Spending money in this way fills us with quite a lot of joy. But when it comes to spending money on things like utilities, electric bills, cell phone bills, water bills or taxes, well this doesn't feel so great. It feels so bad for many people, at some level, deep inside, that it even feels like we are being robbed. It takes us back to when we were children and how it made us feel then. If we keep thinking like this we aren't able to break the cycle and this is what we continue emitting to The Unseen.

So how do we change this way of thinking around as quickly as possible? We do this by changing our entire perspective .We do a complete 360, and instead of resenting the bills that reminded us of our parents' suffering, we change our perception of what we are experiencing in our physical reality at that very moment. We decide no longer to be victims of this situation without any control. We accept that our experiences and conditioning from the past have contributed to our financial lack, but no longer determine our financial future. We relinquish control and decide to become masters of our financial destiny through the power of appreciation.

A change in perspective is easily made when we consider that payment of those bills is a reason for us to be grateful. The mortgage or rent we pay for the homes we live in, which is supplied with electricity and enables us to live and be entertained is worth paying for. The computer and telephone you use for work or to connect with friends and the rest of the world, means you are living in an abundant world already . The fact that you CAN pay these things says much more than you realize. It is when you focus on this that you release yourself from the trauma of the past.

  The very essence of not appreciating paying for the amenities you have at your very fingertips, are the continuing causes of your financial pain. Yes, they do cost money, but doesn't it bring you so much in return? If your focus has more to do with what you are paying for, rather than what you are receiving, then you have no appreciation of money and this is the cause of your financial blueprint being one of lack, as an adult today.

  We have all been pained by youthful encounters with money of which some are due to what we saw our parents experience, but we must help ourselves by taking on new outlooks towards money. We must create them in our minds eye in order to be able to receive them. We must tell ourselves that there is no shortage of money in this universe and that the universe wants us to experience as much as we can. The universe understand that for certain experiences, money is required. Our financial attraction is determined by our financial blueprint. The blueprint we developed as children is not static. It can always be changed and we have the power to do this as adults.

  If your ideas are that money is something bad and something that results in hardship, then simply said, you have to change your thinking. As long as you think this you will never have enough and your financial blueprint will always be pointed away from you, instead of towards you. Once you understand that the flow of money is determined by how you think about, experience and emotionalize money, you will be able to change your financial potential to that of your desires. If we understand the workings of The Unseen, then we must come to realize that it holds just a much potential of money to be gained as it does of your ideas of money to be lacking. The more we focus on the money we don't have, the more it remains elusive to us. The more we think of our fears from the past, the more money avoids us.

Tools
Here are some tips and tools for improving your financial blueprint.

1 – Money is not your master, it's just a tool. Don't let money take control over you. As long as you view money as something that will make your life better, you will always be chasing after it. It's a bit like chasing after a ghost. The thing you should be chasing after, grab onto and destroy, is your negative thoughts about money. So be honest with yourself, discover how you feel about money and find out where those thoughts/ideas/beliefs come from so that you can release them.

2 – Release your memories and the guilt of your parents suffering from money. This had nothing to do with you. By keeping those deep memories alive, you attract the very thing we don't want. How your parents were with money is no reflection on your own financial possibilities.

2 – Pay everything from your luxuries to your bills with a smile. Being happy about having the ability to pay a bill is underrated. It's important, in every aspect of our lives, that we realize how fortunate we are to be able to pay the bills we have. When you are happy about the money you have, the money you have to pay, the money you have to give others, and then realize that you spending money is helping to circulate money, you attract more money. The important thing is to feel good about the money you give to others in every form. The energy you send out at that moment is one of abundance. If you are feeling abundant you can only receive abundance back.

3 - Decide what you want your financial life to be like. You've probably been worrying too long about how much money you have. If there is one thing worrying is good for, it's helping you acknowledge what you don't want your financial life to be like. But worrying without a plan to acquire more money is a waste of valuable energy. When we talk about your financial blueprint, we speak about the potential of money coming into your life, your heart and your home. So, ask yourself, how much you'd like to earn per month or per year and write down what you'd do with all of that money. Enjoy the process of writing it down. It's important and it helps get over any negative feelings that you have towards money. You have lots of old ways of thinking that will fight with the new ways of thinking. When this happens, acknowledge the feelings, but don't be a part of them. Just observe them, without judgment, and then carry on. Be careful of not tripping yourself up by trying to figure out how you're going to earn the money. Leave that part to The Unseen and focus on only what you've been asked to do.

Affirmations

I have two affirmations for you to choose from this time. I know how difficult the subject of money can be, so choose the affirmation which resonates with how you truly feel. Making affirmations that you don't believe in won't work.

My feelings towards money are changing for the better

Or

My financial blueprint points only towards wealth

◌ℨ

A change in perspective is easily made when we consider that that payment of those bills is also a reason for us to be grateful.

⊂ℨ Chapter 10 ℨ⊃
The Power Of Meditation

Introduction

There is a field in this universe called The Unseen. It's been written about several times in this book and it's the most important place you'll ever be able to connect with. You could call it home. It's the place where dreams are envisioned. It's the place where fear does not exist and it's the home of all creation. It's available to us whenever we want, day or night and wherever we are in the world.

One of the ways we grant ourselves access to The Unseen is through silence. We silence our thoughts and silence the sight of our physical surroundings by closing our eyes. The Unseen is the field of all potential and by connecting with it, we tap into infinite possibilities and allow ourselves the time to focus in on our intentions.

Explanation

Meditation connects our subconscious thoughts – the only thoughts that impact reality with The Unseen. When we meditate, we concentrate and focus fully with our subconscious mind. We silence our conscious thoughts, and by closing our eyes we prevent distraction from external influences. Meditation is necessary in life, not only for deliberate creation but also for peace of mind. Meditating helps us to relax, focus, let go, feel our feelings, listen to our intuition, create, intend and so much more. By tapping into our feelings during meditation, we get a clearer understanding of what our mind and bodies are telling us. We have literally thousands of thoughts a day. So many thoughts that it's difficult to know how many of our thoughts are to our advantage or disadvantage. Through meditation, we allow ourselves to go deep into ourselves and reach those very subtle thoughts which we were unaware of. Meditation is about relaxing and in its purest form, about remembering and connecting with the neglected sides of ourselves.

Meditation can also be used for self-healing. There have been hundreds of studies conducted that prove the amazingly positive effects of meditation. But best of all, meditation is 100% free.

Meditation is the one healing resource that we have with us, all of the time. It is something that nobody can ever take away from us.

Using the silence and solitude that meditation brings, enables us to connect with The Unseen. When we use the silence to visualize, we can get ourselves into an ultimate state, completely in line with all potential. At first, the silence can be strange, especially if we are used to busy environments that provide a lot of distractions. Even people around us, from our partners to our families, distract us from ourselves.

Most people think meditation is just for relaxing, but it is more than that. Beyond relaxation lies infinite creation. Beyond relaxation, through meditation, lies the entrance to The Unseen.

Example

How long have you stayed in a room in your home, without any distractions? How long have you been able to do this? Your answer is likely never. We are hardly ever alone with just our thoughts. We see relaxation as being at home and watching the TV or surfing the net.

We are constantly doing things. But it's in the doing of nothing that brings us in very close contact with whom we really are. It's in the stillness between each breath we take, that we get a grasp of our potential.

If we want to tap into the potential that is waiting and available for us in The Unseen, we have to get comfortable with being alone. Being alone means trusting that you do not need to be constantly entertained by people or electronics. Being alone is allowing solitude into your life. Being alone is not being lonely. Being alone is giving yourself the time to simply be. It is in this perfect state, without demands or judgments, that you connect to The Unseen and the potential that it has available for you.

Scenario

If you've never meditated before, then this will be an interesting experience for you. Firstly, the idea of being in silence is just that.

It's just about being silent, no words, no music, no books, not anything. It's not about not thinking. Many people think that meditation is about silencing your thoughts or turning them off, so to speak. This is impossible to do. Meditation is about observing your thoughts. You will have hundreds of thoughts that come and go. Let them come and let them go. Observe them as a part of yourself during meditation, but you don't need to take part in them. Here lies the difference.

When we meditate, we close our eyes. It's good to breathe very deeply and slowly and this will only help us relax even more. Once you have become a little more experienced, you will notice feeling in a trance-like state. This state is a very relaxed state known as Theta. Theta is a brain wave state of 4-8 Hz. It's the state you reach just before dropping off to sleep. In Theta we are greatly connected to The Unseen. We are no longer thinking consciously, but imagining, feeling and creating subconsciously. It's in this state that we imagine with intention, all of the things that we'd like to achieve or have or experience in our lives. In Theta, we visualize and emotionalize. Our imagination and thoughts can literally take us to anywhere we want to go. There are no limits.

Tools
Here are some tips and tools for meditation that help us achieve access to The Unseen.

1 – Make time, even if only 15 minutes, to be alone in the silence without distractions. It's important to feel who you are and know who you are. You can only do this if there is no one and nothing to distract you. It's important to just do nothing at times.

2 – Meditate daily. Even if only for 10 minutes, the importance is establishing a consistent practice. With the exception of guided or music meditations, no sounds should be permitted. If you are using guided meditations, use headphones that cover your ears completely to prevent distractions. When first starting off with meditation, any sudden noise, which you can't place will work as a distraction for you. Make sure that you breathe deeply throughout your meditation. Visit http://www.theunseen.net/free to download a free guided meditation audio for manifestation and creation.

3 – When you are in a deep relaxed state (Theta), start to visualize how you want your life to be. In Theta state, you should be feeling wonderful. Your body will feel different that normal. Theta feels slightly different for everyone but you will definitely know how Theta feels when you experience it. As you visualize, you will notice how the energy in your body rises. You'll feel warm and comfortable. Stay in this state for as long as you want and focus on all that you want. Let your imagination flow.

4 – Let yourself go, dare yourself to dream. Go where your ideal thoughts of your life take you and ignore the head chatter that may occur. Don't be hard on yourself. If thoughts come up, don't take part, just observe them and then go back to focusing on the life you desire. Make it as big as you dare.

Affirmations
Whatever I can imagine, I can achieve

೫

Beyond relaxation, through meditation, lies the entrance to The Unseen.

ଓଃ Chapter 11 ଓ
Your Outer World Reflects Your Inner State

Introduction

We've all had those moments, when our homes are in a mess. All sorts of things are found lying around from newspapers or magazines to socks and shoes, spread all over the floor. Then we'll have dirty dishes waiting to be washed or loaded into the dishwasher or even our children's toys, which we trip over. If you've ever stepped on a rogue Lego piece, then you know what I mean. The mess takes control of our lives and in a not so positive way.

It's not only in our home that we see these kinds of situations occur. Just think back to the state of your desk in the office. Were there piles of papers everywhere and long lists of things to do? Our homes being untidy often results in us tripping over things. Our desks cluttered with paper often leaves us not being able to find information or documents that we need. Life gets messy when we leave it unattended, like weeds that grow in our gardens that disturb the growth of beautiful flowers. It's a common occurrence. This kind of mess not only consumes physical space, but also mental space. When things are left unattended and in the way, they mess up our flow of energy.

Explanation

If you are able to look objectively at your home or work situation, you will find that in those moments of untidiness, your thoughts were untidy too. Life gets tough at times and in our most stressed of times, we often have too much to do. Our focus is diluted and we try to spread our time and attention over too many things. A lack of focus can also be described as a lack of direction. It creates clutter and confusion. It keeps us trapped at a static level, unable to move on, unable to be free.

Now, let's take this concept to a higher state of consciousness. If we are able to notice that when our homes or desks are a mess, that we too are mentally in a mess, then what kind of effect do you think this is having on the things outside of our homes and offices? Our homes represent a dear part of ourselves – our minds and our hearts.

So if our homes represent our inner thoughts and feelings, what kind of energy are we transmitting about ourselves, our achievements, our relationships or even our own statuses to The Unseen?

Example

Here is an example. When you feel bad about yourself, for whatever reason, others mirror that feeling back to you. It's all part and parcel of being connected to the universe. Everyone is connected and the universe always responds (resonates) with what you are energetically sending it through your thoughts and then via your feelings.

The Unseen, through the Law of Attraction, must offer you the same of what you are transmitting because that is what you are asking for, albeit unwittingly, through the way you feel. The Unseen does not discriminate. It just holds potential. It does not place any judgment on the feelings that you have, whether these are of benefit to you or not. You have free will, so you decide. The Unseen simply delivers.

Scenario

When you have negative thoughts about a person or situation, your emotions respond to that thought and also become negative. You have then taken on those feelings about that person or situation even if it doesn't directly have anything to do with you. Because, as humans we have the habit of internalizing situations (making ourselves a part of it, even if that is not the case), it then become your experience. If you are upset with someone for something they have done, or disappointed with the outcome of a situation, and the thoughts that arise from this are upsetting, then the emotional experience which you are experiencing becomes your experience and your projection. You may think that it is the situation that causes the way you feel, but it is actually your response and your thoughts about the situation which makes you feel the way you do.

It's important to remember that your thoughts determine how you feel. Your thoughts stand free of any situation. You bring your thoughts about a situation into the situation at hand. The situation itself does nothing. It's important to learn to see objectively in cases like this, because by doing so, you unconsciously make yourself a part of the problem, and by doing that you get into the habit of making the situation bigger than it actually is. **You don't think negatively because you feel negative. You feel negative about something because your thoughts have been negative about it**. It's the other way around.

If you want to know how you feel and cannot feel it yourself, then just look at how other people respond to you. They respond in such a way because that is the energy you are offering. It is subtle, that's for sure, but when we look mindfully at what we are thinking, we cannot deny that our feelings are reflected in the events and people around us. Being conscious of this changes our lives the moment we realize it. We have been taught to live in a world of cause and effect. We have been taught that we can only think and feel good if our physical situations around us dictate this and give us evidence to do so. It's the Newtonian way of thinking, but Newton's theories have long been outdated.

Changing the way we think about ourselves, and the people and situations around us, is easy, in theory, but takes time to implement. We're afraid of the word 'difficulty', but we needn't be. Something which is difficult is simply something we don't yet know how to do. Something which is difficult is not something we cannot achieve. The things we experience as being difficult are simply the thing we still need to learn.

Tools
Here are some tips and tools to strengthen your inner world and influence your outer world

1 – Turn off your instinctive responses to things. A lot of what we do comes from habits that have been wired in our brains. If we do the same thing time and time again, it becomes a habit. It's the way babies learn. They repeat things again and again and before your know it, they're walking. But this way of doing things can serve us detrimentally too. When you find yourself in an uncomfortable situation, simply try to respond differently. If you would normally get angry, for example, try instead to take a few deep breaths before responding. If you do this, you'll most likely respond differently and more so in the way that you want to, rather than the way you would automatically do.

2 – Take responsibility for your inner world. This means that you need to acknowledge when you are tired, stressed or moody. You don't have to be a slave to the way you automatically think or the way you think you feel. You need to be kinder to yourself and in doing this, others will be kinder to you. You are the mirror.

3 – Tidy up your home or desk. You live in a place where you should be able to come home and relax. It's difficult to relax when there are all kinds of distractions around you. An untidy home is an untidy mind and often when you tidy up you experience a clearing and clarity of the mind. You will think good thoughts about what you have achieved and this in return will make you feel good inside.

4 – Make it a practice to reduce clutter. Putting things back where they belong, after you have used them brings peace of mind. Just think about it, you'll never have to search for the bottle opener or your keys, knowing it's in a safe place. Peace of mind brings clarity, structure and order and this leaves you with the feeling of being in control of your life and your choices.

Affirmation
My mind is clear and I have space to be.

C3

If you want to know how you feel and cannot feel it yourself, then just look at how other people respond to you.

ℭ Chapter 12 ℭ
How To Manifest Your Dream Life And Get It When You Want It

Introduction

There is nothing in this universe that you cannot have. There is nothing in this universe that you seek, that doesn't seek you. We have been put on this earth as humans with the objective of experiencing life and everything that life has to offer. Isn't that a wonderful idea! But it's not just an idea, it's the truth and nothing but the truth.

This universe can only experience human life through us. Other forms of life are being experienced all of the time. Just look at nature, and how it effortlessly exists. A tree does not struggle to be a tree, it just is, and even when what we perceive as its death - the leaves falling off and its seeds falling to the ground - life continues to be expressed. The cycle never ends. The seeds from the trees are blown through the winds and land again on the earth. The process of creation simply begins anew through the earth's soil – a tree is born, yet again.

The universe does not treat nature any differently to how it treats people. The same opportunities are available. We have the privilege of being conscious and aware. We get to create our lives and we do this through our thoughts and feelings.

Everything is available to us without limitation, and yet so many of us don't dare to dream, imagine or even have thoughts of a life of abundance and happiness. Even if it is given to us on a silver platter, which it is, we are simply too afraid of going for the ultimate.

Explanation

The world we live in is abundant. There is never a shortage of what is available and there is so much available that it's actually difficult to comprehend. It is omnipotent. Omnipotence means having an indefinite or unlimited amount of power, potential or possibilities. This is a difficult concept to grasp because we have been told otherwise. We have been told that there is a limit to everything, that we must 'enjoy it while it lasts' which is also a complete contradiction. To enjoy it while it lasts means that something is going to end. As soon as we understand this, the enjoyment is destroyed. We end up focusing and fearing the end.

If we have been conditioned, through society , to believe that there is shortage and lack, then there will be shortage and lack. If shortage and lack is our expectation and our feeling, then that is what we will receive. Now, some of you may now be wondering how this can be when there is so much poverty and hardship in the world. You may think that starving people have never asked for the shortage and lack they are experiencing. This is true and this is certainly a reality for many, but the situations that cause poverty and hardships are man-made. If we have free will, which we all do, we have the free will to cause and create hardships not only for ourselves but for others also. Just because the universe is abundant does not mean that the universe will clean up our mess. The poverty we see on earth was created by man and needs to be resolved by man. It is not the fault of God, source, the divine or universal intelligence. It was not created by the concept of any of these. It was created by us and the responsibility needs to be taken by us, collectively.

Example

What you see in the media, most of the time, is a bad representation of how life really is. Most still believe that Africa is a poor dark land where people are starving and diseases prevail. Factually and scientifically speaking, you couldn't be further from the truth. The media is great at giving bad news and rarely interested in good news. We are so influenced by what the media tells us that we take it as truth and this becomes a part of our belief system and ultimately forms the way we look at the world. This contributes to how our realities are shaped.

We have to help ourselves by changing our points of view, changing our thoughts and remembering that there are always possibilities. We need to accept the idea that for every challenge there is a solution.

Scenario

What does a dream life look like? It will look different to each one of us. What one person defines as happiness could quite easily be a nightmare for someone else. There are some people whose idea of a dream life is living close to nature and having no obligations. For another person, their idea of a dream life would be to live as close as possible to the hustle and bustle of a big city. Whatever you desire in your life, you do need to be clear on it. It has to be defined. It won't just fall into your lap. This means you have to ask yourself what kind of life you desire and really go into detail with it. It also means that you'll have to take the steps towards that life as if you knew you already had it. **It means moving forward in the direction of your dreams and meeting it at the other end.**

It's difficult to do. How can we imagine that life is truly different that it shows itself to be? Even if you do manage to make steps in the direction of your dream life, you'll have to do it on faith. Where's the proof in that? Although faith is a spiritual concept, quantum physics confirms that our feelings and thoughts are the things that create our physical realities. Science now says that anything you think about you also have the potential to bring about. If thinking and feelings come first, then you have only faith to rely on for its physical manifestation. Perhaps you were hoping that science would tell you otherwise. Perhaps you were hoping for a scientific explanation that would fit in with the idea of cause and effect. Well, I'm sorry to disappoint you. Quantum physics simply proves that physical manifestation is the result of thought and feeling waves in our universe.

Tools

Here are some tips and tools on help you manifest your dream life.

1 – Question your belief system. Is what you believe really true, or have you heard it so many times that you've never challenged the idea and taken it on as your own belief?

2 – Make a commitment to write down your ideal life. It doesn't matter if it sounds silly. You have to start somewhere and it won't happen unless you start to get clear on what you want out of life. Create a journal and add to it whenever you get new ideas or want new things.

3 – Delve into the world of Quantum Physics. There are plenty of books for you to read to help you in this understanding and acceptance of it. I've included a list in the appendix.

4 – Don't let other people's ideas influence yours. This new way of thinking is a total shock to how we have understood life. Don't look for support outside of yourself, you'll likely be laughed at or people simply will not be able to understand this without 'proof'.

Affirmation
I allow myself to lead the life I truly desire

✂

Everything is available to us without limitation, and yet so many of us don't dare to dream, imagine or even have thoughts of a life of abundance and happiness.

ℭଃ Epilogue ଣ

When you hit rock bottom, the only way is up... but you don't ever have to hit rock bottom!

Some years ago, I went through a major disruption in my life. Literally everything was falling apart. My marriage ended in a bitter divorce, my living situation was unstable, my business had literally died and I felt as if almost everyone around me had deserted me. My family was the greatest support but they all lived far away. I had very few friends left. I had already delved into the world of the universe and successfully used the Law of Attraction, but there was something I didn't quite understand about how the universe worked. I had no concept of The Unseen or how important my feelings were in the process of creating the life I wanted. You see, I'd always believed that if you want something you had to work hard for it.

I believed that the road to success was fraught with complications, and that success didn't necessarily include happiness. I was having positive thoughts, but these thoughts were not supported by positive feelings. Instead, they were supported by the idea that positive thinking still meant extreme working conditions, conflicts and struggles. I had assumed that success was possible but also meant competition, jealousy, difficulties and struggle. Looking back, this way of thinking didn't make sense and even when it wasn't serving me, my ignorance stopped me from taking a step back to look at my life and question my thoughts. How can we have positive thoughts about one thing but expect hardships at the same time? Where is the logic in that kind of thinking? Well, there is no logic in it.

I had taken on a new life philosophy but was still chained to old beliefs. I was transmitting contradictory energy into The Unseen, and my emotions were more strongly tied to the experience of success with hardships, than the positive thoughts I was having.

My conditioning and beliefs have been built up since childhood. These are strong and intense feelings and emotions which framed my point of view. The new way of thinking was a new belief which still needed to gather strength and conviction. In no way could my positive thinking outweigh 35+ years of conditioning and deep subconscious limiting beliefs, and so I hit rock bottom. I had fought with all my might to improve my situation, but things just didn't work out.

The strange thing that happens in such a situation, is that its only when we hit rock bottom that we can then rise back up. The act of surrendering gave me great power. I couldn't see it then, but as soon as I had accepted the situation as it was, I realized what it was that I was actually experiencing and at that point everything began to change.

I didn't have to wait months or years for the change, in fact, everything got better within a number of weeks. Although I was still in the formal stages of divorce, I had found a new house to live in and began to work as a consultant. My business was ruined, at least formally. In truth the collapse of the business meant that certain unhealthy parts of the business were stopped in their tracks and I could start the business again. I did just that and my new business became significantly more successful.

In retrospect, I see how I created the destruction of some very fundamental parts of my life to discover and experience an even better life. You see, the universe knows what is best for us and the pain I had experienced in that time, was simply my resistance to a change which was inevitable for a better future. I didn't want to see my marriage or business failing. I didn't want to move home and move my children because it would mean uprooting not only my life, but that of my children too. I was too proud to ask for help and this meant that my experiences only became more difficult. I didn't have to hit rock bottom but I did create it.

Allowing

There is an important aspect of working in alignment with The Unseen, and that is the art of allowing. The art of allowing is the ability to allow yourself to experience better times or a better or greater life. The idea of this being possible is the knowing that this is, and will always be, a potential possibility for us. We can get into good contact with ourselves about this by asking ourselves these questions:

Do I think I deserve happiness?
Do I think I deserve a better life?
Do I think I'm a good person?

These are potent questions that we rarely ask ourselves, but if you answer them honestly, you'll get a deep insight into what you allow or disallow yourself in life.

Blocks

We hold a resistance in ourselves emotionally when times are tough. What I mean by this is that, when we are experiencing difficulty, we tend to not want to experience the pain that comes with that difficulty, so we block our emotions off. We become hardened about it and this puts us into a bad mood.

This block doesn't actually help us, although we think it does. What this block does, is block everything, including the things we need or the things which are good for us. It doesn't actually block only the bad stuff. It increases the negative stuff and makes us feel worse. We think we are protecting ourselves when we turn this block on, but we're not at all.

The art of allowing enables us to go through the feelings brought on by the thoughts about a situation. Like my disruption some years ago, it was not so much the situation which caused the emotional difficulty, but more so my resistance to the situation- my blocking the feelings that came alone with it. It made me hard, but it didn't help me. I wasn't allowing myself to experience what was happening, but I needed to experience that in order to go through it. I learnt the hard way, but I didn't need to. If I had listened to my feelings then the huge transition I went through may have been easier. The outcome wouldn't have changed, that I am sure of because the place it brought me to is far better than where I was.

The universe had better plans for me and it always knows the best way to get there. We just have to let it do it work by making it clear which things we are prepared to allow into our lives. After that, all we then have to do is have faith in The Unseen!

‎ Appendix ‎

The following lists a selection of articles, books and resources used as inspiration for this book.

They include spiritual principles as well as scientific papers and research documents that provide for a deeper understanding of how our universe works, how The Unseen delivers and how the Law of Attraction communicates and plays a role in our lives.

Breaking the habit of being you – Dr. Joe Dispenza
Life and Spirit in the Quantum Field – Doug Bennett
The Biology of Belief – Bruce Lipton PhD
Your invisible power – Genevieve Behrend
How to worry less about Money – John Armstrong
The Law of Divine Compensation – Marianne Williamson
The Essential Einstein – Stephan Hawkings
The Laws Underlying The Physics of Everyday Life Are Completely Understood (article) – Sean Carroll
Bioenergetics Field – University of Hawaii at Manoa, Victor J. Stenger
Physics and Psychics: The Search for a World Beyond the Senses - Victor J. Stenger
Gapminder.org (website)
The Hidden messages in water – Masuro Emoto
The Power of Now – Eckhart Tolle
Visual Motor Rehearsal - Dr. Denis Waitley

Did you enjoy this (e)book? If so, please leave a review on Amazon via the following links:

Amazon: amzn.to/1JTCv6f

Reviews are extremely important for new authors. Your comment and rating is greatly appreciated!

ℭ About the Author ℬ

Moriam S. Balogun has written hundreds of articles about the spiritual universe and its effect on human life. Her passion for understanding how perception shapes reality led her to start a Facebook community in 2013 where she shared insights about the principles of the indescribable world we live in.

Within a period of 2 years, after creating a second community, her total reach had climbed to 100.000 people world-wide and continues to grow today. Moriam offers community members one-to-one coaching sessions where she explains in further detail how we can learn to help the universe work in our favor and align ourselves in perfect match with our desires.

Moriam was born in London, United Kingdom but has been living in Amsterdam, The Netherlands, since 1997. She is also fluent in Dutch, has 3 children and lives with her partner Jeroen.

Aside from her passion for The Unseen, Moriam has a strong love of coffee, wine and smelly cheeses preferably paired with a few explicable moments in silence. By day, Moriam is an entrepreneur and investor specialized in online digital businesses.

For more information visit: http://www.theunseen.net

19486229R00080

Printed in Great Britain
by Amazon